This Workbook Belongs To: ________

Own Your Shift
Workbook & Journal

A Companion Guide

HOLLI PEEL

100X PUBLISHING

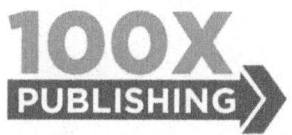

Own Your Shift Workbook & Journal
© 2022 Holli Peel

Published by 100X Publishing
Olympia, Washington | www.100xPublishing.com

All rights reserved. No part of this publication may be reproduced, stored in a retrieval system, or transmitted in any form or by any means--for example, electronic, photocopy, printed out or emailed/distributed to others, recording--without the prior written permission of the publisher.

Scripture quotations marked TPT are from The Passion Translation®. Copyright © 2017, 2018, 2020 by Passion & Fire Ministries, Inc. Used by permission. All rights reserved. ThePassionTranslation.com.

The Holy Bible, English Standard Version. ESV® Text Edition: 2016. Copyright © 2001 by Crossway Bibles, a publishing ministry of Good News Publishers.

Holy Bible, New Living Translation, copyright © 1996, 2004, 2015 by Tyndale House Foundation. Used by permission of Tyndale House Publishers, Inc., Carol Stream, Illinois 60188. All rights reserved.

ISBN: 978-1-7339893-6-7

Cover design by Lyss Aviles

Contents

Introduction	5
How to Use This Workbook & Journal	8
The Shift of Awareness	12
The Shift of Support	23
The Shift of Perseverance	32
The Shift of Gratitude	41
The Shift of Self	50
The Shift of Obedience	62
The Shift of Story	73
The Shift of Celebration	83
What's Next?	93
About the Author	99

Introduction

There is something thrilling about getting a fresh journal; it feels like a fresh start of endless possibilities. There have been many times I've hesitated to embark on the journey of what is possible for the sake of keeping the journal fresh and clean. In my mind, a messy, full journal was no longer open to possibilities.

In doing this I have missed out on many explorations of myself by keeping the journal "nice and tidy." Now more than ever I'm convinced that journals are meant to be messy. They are meant to be keepers of our sacred processes; they are meant to capture and hold the keys and breakthroughs for future seasons.

I hope you won't make the same mistake I have in the past of cherishing the possibilities instead of taking them head on and working them out with a process. Our individual process is so sacred; it's our own personal invitation to do life with our Creator. To miss the opportunity to document that, even in the most simple of ways, is devastating.

My prayer for this journal is that you would allow it to be a safe place while you're in the messy middle of life. There is never a season when journaling is a bad idea. Many truths and breakthroughs await you in the process of working it out with a pen and paper.

In my book Own Your Shift, there are sections to take you through tangible experiences, giving you the opportunity to encounter your Creator and to learn more about who He created you to be.

It is said that in times of trial people are often "made," and there are two core outcomes:
1. You become a stronger, more insightful, and well-rounded person, or
2. You grow in frustration and resentment, allowing your life experiences to let bitterness sink in.

My goal in putting these tools together for you is so you will have resources at your disposal for every season of your life. In hard times, I want you to know how to take action and shift yourself continuously into the best version of yourself - into the original design and intent your Creator had when He intricately and delicately wove (or knitted, based on translation used) you together. Let's take a look at this truth in Psalm 139:13 in two different translations.

The Passion Translation (TPT): *You formed my innermost being, shaping my delicate inside and my intricate outside, and <u>wove</u> them all together in my mother's womb.*

New Living Translation (NLT): *You made all the delicate, inner parts of my body and <u>knit</u> me together in my mother's womb.*

You can use this journal in tandem with the book or use it separately. Both are equally as powerful, especially when you use your experience and truth as awareness points on your map of THE TRUTH. What do I mean by that?

Well, I never want you to sell your life experiences short. After all, everything you have experienced and been through has shaped you into the person you are today, so I never want to ignore or shame where we have come from as individuals.

However, just because we experienced something, and it is our current truth, it doesn't mean that it is THE TRUTH.

For example, my truth for the longest time was I can never finish something I start. I would always get burnt out and tired of doing the same thing over and over for the result I was looking for, but just because it was my experience and truth at the time, never finishing things was not and is not THE TRUTH.

Jesus is the person of Truth, and He is the Finisher. He lived a finished life; He completed all He came to achieve, and His finished work of the cross is actually my truth as well. I just need to come to a place where I am ready to let my old truth die on the cross with Him like He said it did. Only when I can find peace in the person I was can I become the person He made me to be...

If I'm being honest, I never thought my book would be finished; I never thought it would be published, but here it is! I took on the TRUTH of who HE is IN me and became a finisher!

I share this with you because I want you to get in the practice of seeing where you are now. Feel it; allow it to be true, but don't let yourself stay there. Why? Because there is so much more available to you in the Truth of Jesus. How will you show up in life when you know shifting from stuck to success is just on the other side of taking ownership and knowing what is available to you?

My prayer is that you take pride in owning your experience here on earth. You can have a say in how it goes. Yes, I know the Lord orders our steps, but we partner with Him. What I mean by that is no matter the season—hard times, great times, and everything in between—our attitude toward the season is what truly "controls" our experience.

For example, in the midst of chaos and what feels like a very challenging season, I will press into JOY. I know there is a popular statement floating around that says I can do hard things. Of course, that is true; we can all do hard things. After all, we have all made it through 100% of our hard days, right? But let's take that a step further...instead of suffering through the hard things, instead of gritting our teeth and just pushing through, what if we add "with joy" to it? Say it with me:

"I can do hard things, with JOY!"

This is how you get to have control and have a say in your life. So change your attitude, your level of ownership of self, and stewardship of the season the Lord has you in.

How empowering is it to know we can shift the results of the "hard things" in our lives? For me it is life changing. It took me from depressed, broken, hurting, miserable, and lacking all confidence to thriving, vibrant, successful, and full enjoyment.

Hard things still come my way, but I choose to greet them differently, and that's the power of this companion guide to Own Your Shift. It, too, will help walk you through and give you tangible tools on how to do the same - how to shift yourself from feeling stuck where you are to thriving where you want to be. Change your mind, heal your heart, gain understanding of WHOSE you are and who He is, and then your whole life can flip upside down in all the right ways.

Who will you become in the pages of this journal? What secrets will your Creator and the Truth reveal to you? What keys from Heaven will you get to help unlock breakthroughs for yourself and others?

The possibilities are endless when you dive in! Are you ready to Own Your Shift? These pages are all yours, so fill them in with your process, no matter how messy. Enjoy!

How to Use This Workbook & Journal

This workbook and journal's sections correspond with my main book, Own Your Shift. I have included brief summaries of each shift that's discussed in the book, along with questions, exercises, declarations, and more, plus space for you to journal and draw as you process through it with God. Use this as a true companion to help you through the book. I believe the book and companion guide will be a tool in your life, giving you the ability to come back as often as needed for your human experience.

There is no denying that as people, our journey is messy; there are emotions and feelings that could easily lead us astray if we are not willing to identify them and work through them. One suggestion would be to go through this process once a quarter. Each time you come back to this tool, make note of how your answers change and what God is talking to you about in the current season.

There is always fresh revelation available to us.
There is always a deeper level of healing available to us.
There is always an invitation from Papa God to upgrade.

Use this journal as a way to document your process and to go on a discovery journey. Allow yourself to get messy and be in process. Be proud of yourself for showing up and being willing to do the hard work. Not everyone is willing to get messy or become undignified in the process of becoming your truest and most authentic brilliant creation, but for those who are willing to go on the journey, the reward is rich and oh so worth it.

Here is a list of the sections and their purposes:

This Is the Shift of...

Each section lists which shift we'll be working on and what you can expect to gain. All eight shifts were key lessons I had to learn to heal and move into a deeper level of my God-given authority and purpose. You may have encounters and memories of your own with each of these shifts at different points in your life. Along with a brief description and explanation of the shift, I may also share some personal stories and examples from my life to help you relate and to identify scenarios you may have experienced as well. What God is willing to do for one, He is willing to do for another. Let the testimony of His presence in my life remind you that He is present in yours as well. He's in every tiny detail and the major core memories too.

Ask Questions

Use this section to deepen your awareness and understanding of your own shift as it's taking place. Questions help direct our thoughts, and they bring light to places within us that we might not think to go on our own. I encourage you to journal and sit with these questions. Revisit them as often as necessary. I also encourage you not to judge your first or next answer. There is always a process, and questions are a beautiful invitation to unwind or untangle old thoughts, mindsets, heart postures, or patterns. Questions are a beautiful gift. In the New Testament, you will notice how Jesus almost always answers a question with another question. If my question doesn't spark anything for you, how can you reword it to be what you need to answer? If you pose a better question, post it and tag me on Instagram or DM me.

Tangible Tools

I believe there is power in tangible things. If we were only spiritual beings, God wouldn't have given us bodies or an earth to enjoy. I don't think Jesus would have come in the form of man if there was no value in showing up tangibly. The tangible tools I will share have been used in my journey and healing. I love tangible things that go beyond a mental process or spiritual encounters. I use nature, essential oils, journals, and mementos of moments when God moved in my life.

However, things should never replace the Person. If anything distracts you from God or pulls you away from Him, it's not right in this season for you. For example, I went through a season when God asked me to discard my massive rock collection. I said yes because He asked. He later brought them back into my life because He knows I enjoy them, but I was willing to surrender them. You have to know your season. You have to know He is the Source, and tangible things are only resources from the Source.

Tangible items in our life can and do serve important purposes and meanings, but the key is to never let them rise above the Source who allowed these items into our lives. So, you'll see the hands-on activities, things, and suggestions I share, but I trust that you have the Holy Spirit to help you know the season you're in. None of these suggestions are in stone; they are all "editable" to what fits you.

The Sounds of His Voice

Scripture is one of my favorite tangible tools. I believe God allows us to experience Scripture in different ways at different times. He gives us the honor of pressing into His Word to see deeper levels of revelation and to see how He is living in His Word right now. These verses are passages that spoke to me about the shifts, and I hope they speak to you too. Explore the scriptures I include, and use the space provided to journal about it. I always encourage you to add more scriptures that speak to you, or use the same scripture and give it more depth and context in your personal life and experiences.

Learning Forward

Here's a radical thought: celebrating failure and mistakes is important. You can start to see "failure" with fresh eyes. There is never a failure, just a missed opportunity to learn. You can choose to learn forward, to see "failures" as invitations to lean in and learn forward in any and all circumstances. This was one of my greatest lessons. I used to be gripped with fear of failure, and when I accepted that failure was the "goal" so I could keep learning forward, I realized it was no longer scary. It was actually something that gave me permission to take action and try because there were never "mistakes," just opportunities. It's amazing how many times you will succeed when you put fear of failure to the side and go for it anyway. Learning Forward will have some questions for you to ponder and journal about.

Breathwork

Our breath is powerful, sacred, and God-given. When we can intentionally focus on our breath, it is a divine connection to our Creator. I love the picture painted in Ezekiel 37. I know there are theological debates about it being a vision or not, but regardless, the power of breath brings things to life. God used it to create Adam. It is flow, it is empowering, it is wind that brings life. So, when we intentionally focus on our breath, it helps us come back in line and awaken life that is already within us.

Ezekiel 37:4-10 (NIV): Then he said to me, "Prophesy to these bones and say to them, 'Dry bones, hear the word of the Lord! This is what the Sovereign Lord says to these bones: I will make breath enter you, and you will come to life. I will attach tendons to you and make flesh come upon you and cover you with skin; I will put breath in you, and you will come to life. Then you will know that I am the Lord.'" Then he said to me, "Prophesy to the breath; prophesy, son of man, and say to it, 'This is what the Sovereign Lord says: Come, breath, from the four winds and breathe into these slain, that they may live.'" So I prophesied as he commanded me, and breath entered them; they came to life and stood up on their feet—a vast army.

Also, the Holy Spirit has been described as the breath of God, so as you breathe in, imagine breathing the Holy Spirit into every cell of your being. Tools are here to help us draw closer to God in every way. I am not a certified breathwork facilitator, although I have participated in many breathwork sessions. But more than that, I have allowed God to speak to me about my breath, Him as the Breath of Life, and what it looks like to let Him flow through me (my lungs). I say this because I want to encourage the same for you. I will give you examples of breath exercises that have helped me, but I want you to give yourself permission to edit or alter my suggestions to what best suits you. Allow this to be an opportunity to feel and experience His Spirit filling you and being in your physical body. Allow Him to encounter you, right where you are, with these practices, and then write down what you experienced.

Visualizing

Visualizing is the practice of being able to see, not with sight, but with vision. It's a function of the heart, and as you get your heart healthy in the process, you will start to see things birthed and come to life.

> "Vision is the source and hope of life. The greatest gift ever given to mankind is not the gift of sight, but the gift of vision. Sight is a function of the eyes; vision is a function of the heart. Eyes that look are common, but eyes that see are rare. Nothing noble or noteworthy on earth was ever done without vision." —Myles Munroe

"Purpose is when you know and understand what you were born to accomplish. Vision is when you see it in your mind and begin to imagine it." —Myles Munroe

The vision exercises in this book are examples of how you can practice "seeing" in your mind and give you perspective on what is possible when you partner with God for the vision He created you with. He has it all for you; it's a matter of you starting to see and believe the beautiful vision that He already knows is possible for your life.

Declarations and Decrees

Declarations announce to the world what's to come. Your decree is the what's to come, the order, the official stamp of "I know that I know." These are different from affirmations, though they may seem similar. Affirmations serve as an attempt to convince yourself of who you are. Decrees come from a place of knowing the truth unequivocally and declaring it. Most of these decrees are scriptures or variations of a scripture.

Luke 4:18: "The Spirit of the Lord is upon me, because he has anointed me to proclaim good news to the poor. He has sent me to proclaim liberty to the captives and recovery of sight to the blind, to see at liberty those who are oppressed." This is an example of us being empowered to proclaim or declare the good news. Sometimes we are the captives, poor, blind, or oppressed, and we need to declare in our own lives the good news that God empowered us with.

Job 22:28: "You will decide on a matter, and it will be established for you, and light will shine on your ways." Like I said, part of decreeing is "knowing that you know." Believe His Word for what has been ALREADY given to you. Simply believe it so you can easily take action and allow His already-established truth and blessings to thrive in your daily life.

Be sure to use this companion guide to fill in any extra decrees that apply to your specific situation and life. Allow them to become your prayers and thanksgiving to your Creator for all He has already said yes and amen to.

With each of these sections, my prayer is that your vision expands, that you are able to see more of what your Creator has in store for you, and you start believing it to be true in a new and fresh way. Reading this book won't be enough though; your courage to take action on the words within these pages is what will bring change to your life.

So, are you ready? Let's dive in, friend! Be sure to tag me on Instagram while you're working on your companion guide @hollipeel. I want to cheer you on and celebrate you in the hard and in the easy times. XO

The Shift of Awareness

First things first, we need the Shift of Awareness. This journey starts with becoming aware of what's really going on around us, what we have inside of us, and who we really are. This shift can be a tricky one to navigate because our level of awareness can easily become clouded by our circumstances. We can mistakenly identify what is going on around us as a "me problem" or a "them problem" without accurately taking ownership of our role. No matter how messy the growth might be, it's important to stay committed to the process of becoming, the process of shifting, the process of what God has in store for us.

Without being aware of ourselves—our emotions, feelings, and actions—a treacherous journey to experiencing freedom awaits us. But it doesn't have to be that way. Instead, we can develop awareness tools and use them to practice living in the freedom God has given us, particularly on the inside!

In life, there are some conversations and situations when unexpected things come up within us: pangs of pain, reactions, and sudden emotions. These triggers are meant to help our awareness. They show us that we are wounded and not fully experiencing God's freedom in a specific area. These incredibly uncomfortable moments challenge and test us.

Let's compare awareness to photo filters on Instagram. Through what lenses do you see situations in your life? How do you interpret what goes on around you? Do you recognize that others interact with you through their filters as well? Our filters change our perspective, for better or worse, but we must understand something: we may not see what's real and true. Our version of truth could be off a bit, missing major facts, or be dead wrong. Some of our filters might be shame, distrust, fear, or rejection. When we become aware of our filters, we can practice responding to our triggers with wisdom instead of reacting haphazardly. Awareness is the first step in harnessing power over our filters and triggers.

With self-awareness, we learn to control the timing of our filters. When my son Micah decides to swing his arms freely, without a care, an open field is the perfect place and timing to do so. But in a crowded room, the timing is 100% wrong, and flailing his arms about would be unsafe for himself and others. Maybe your life always feels like a crowded room. We can be 100% correct that the life experiences we've had and the trauma we've endured rightfully compels us to protect ourselves. However, we can be 100% wrong about guarding ourselves against every single person on the planet. We can be 100% right and 100% wrong at the same time…no wonder we often feel confused and overwhelmed!

Learning who you are is healing.
Learning who you are is awareness.
Learning who you are gives God so much glory.
Now, let's work on this together and write some things down…

Ask Questions

In the past week, what types of situations have provoked intense and uncomfortable emotions in me?

___

Can I recognize any patterns? Are the emotions usually similar or different depending on the circumstances?

___

Am I having a difficult time seeing situations for what they are? Are my emotions so intense that recognizing my triggers evades me? What kind(s) of situations does this happen in?

___

Am I willing to admit that having blind spots is common for people with heart wounds? Can I give myself permission to become aware and accept my current emotional condition?

___

Will I choose to trust God's mercy and rely on Him to lift the emotional burden as I adopt a posture of awareness? When I am fully trusting God, what does it feel like and how do I show up in life?

_____
_____
_____
_____
_____

How am I experiencing myself in this new posture of awareness? Do my emotions feel different? Does my body feel the same? What is the pace and content of my thoughts?

_____
_____
_____
_____
_____

Whether I'm noticing subtle or significant changes, what is one way I can be still and rest in what God is doing in me in this moment?

_____
_____
_____
_____

Am I getting a tiny, gentle glimpse of a new perspective on my wounds and triggers? Or maybe God is brightly flashing a giant new vision? How can I take note and choose awareness of this new perspective?

_____
_____
_____

How will I express gratitude and love to God for what He shows me in this shift?

_____
_____
_____

Tangible Tools

As you ask yourself the questions above, consider walking or moving your body in some way. Sometimes physical movement facilitates emotional and spiritual movement. Think about the people in Scripture! Much learning and change took place while people were on the move. They didn't drive cars and sit behind desks or in front of screens all day!

Talk to God as you move. Listen as you move. See how your body feels.

Where is it tight in my body? Where do I need to come into alignment physically?

_____

_____

_____

As you align physically, you will see that your spirit and soul also come into deeper alignment. Our bodies carry the experiences in life, so when we slow down to listen to our bodies, we find deeper levels of potential healing.

Ask for a hug from someone you love. If you don't have someone near you, wrap your arms around yourself and embrace. Happy hormones are released in your body when you are embraced. The shift of awareness is challenging – you're doing hard work! A physical feeling of love and affection that comes from a hug communicates to your body that you are safe and secure (in other words, the opposite of our fight-or-flight response).

The Sounds of His Voice

> Every section of this workbook and journal includes The Sounds Of His Voice - a section from the main book that has scriptures to read. God is so good that He hard wired us to hear and experience His voice. There are four primary ways to encounter the voice of God, and I will describe those briefly. Before I do, I want you to know that God built you with multiple senses, and you can encounter Him through each of them. Yes, you can taste, see, hear, feel, and smell, and seeing, hearing, and feeling are three of the core ways to encounter God. The fourth is "knowing."
>
> How do you know which you are?
>
> 1. If you are a "feeler," you might be highly emotional or strongly feel the emotions of others. You might walk into a room or atmosphere and feel emotions you were not feeling before you

walked in, picking up on other people's emotions. Some people call this "empath," which is really just a strong gift or ability to be empathetic toward others, actually feeling what they are going through. This is my primary way to experience God and my fellow humans. It was tricky growing up because I really thought I was crazy. In reality, I just needed to understand and hone my gift.

2. If you are a "seer," you get visions, you find yourself daydreaming, or have vivid dreams at night. Maybe it's easy for you to see pictures that others describe with words. If you close your eyes, you are able to imagine images in your mind's eye. There are many great books out about this topic. A couple of my favorites are The Veil by Blake K. Healy and Seer by James W. Goll. The Lord might speak to you through pictures; ask Him and explore what those pictures mean. The Lord might even speak to you through movies, TV shows, or media.

3. If you are a "hearer," you might find yourself thinking about your thoughts. Language and words are important to you; it might really matter to you how people use words, and you could even be a grammar buff. Maybe you find that the Lord speaks strongly to you through reading or hearing sermons.

4. If you are a "knower," you are one who trusts your gut and intuition. You lean strongly into "I know because I know." You don't always know how you know certain things, but you are typically right and accurate when you follow your intuition.

Now that you know a little more about identifying how you hear His voice, write down what you believe are your primary and secondary ways to experience Him.

_____
_____
_____
_____
_____

With this new awareness, use it throughout this journal and workbook to go deeper in sharpening that gift into a true skill set of hearing God's voice for your life. You can carry this into the rest of this book.

Here is The Sounds of His Voice verse for this chapter to read and listen for His voice:

Psalm 139 (TPT)

You Know All About Me
For the Pure and Shining One
King David's poetic song

Lord, you know everything there is to know about me.
You perceive every movement of my heart and soul,
and you understand my every thought before it even enters my mind.
You are so intimately aware of me, Lord.
You read my heart like an open book and you know all the words I'm about to speak before I even start a sentence!
You know every step I will take before my journey even begins.
You've gone into my future to prepare the way,
and in kindness you follow behind me to spare me from the harm of my past.
You have laid your hand on me!
This is just too wonderful, deep, and incomprehensible!
Your understanding of me brings me wonder and strength.
Where could I go from your Spirit?
Where could I run and hide from your face?
If I go up to heaven, you're there!
If I go down to the realm of the dead, you're there too!
If I fly with wings into the shining dawn, you're there!
If I fly into the radiant sunset, you're there waiting!
Wherever I go, your hand will guide me;
your strength will empower me.
It's impossible to disappear from you or to ask the darkness to hide me, for your presence is everywhere, bringing light into my night.
There is no such thing as darkness with you.
The night, to you, is as bright as the day;
there's no difference between the two.
You formed my innermost being, shaping my delicate inside and my intricate outside, and wove them all together in my mother's womb.
I thank you, God, for making me so mysteriously complex!
Everything you do is marvelously breathtaking.
It simply amazes me to think about it!
How thoroughly you know me, Lord!
You even formed every bone in my body when you created me in the secret place;
carefully, skillfully you shaped me from nothing to something.
You saw who you created me to be before I became me!
Before I'd ever seen the light of day,
the number of days you planned for me were already recorded in your book.
Every single moment you are thinking of me!
How precious and wonderful to consider that you cherish me constantly in your every thought!
O God, your desires toward me are more than the grains of sand on every shore!

When I awake each morning, you're still with me.
O God, come and slay these bloodthirsty, murderous men!
For I cry out, "Depart from me, you wicked ones!"
See how they blaspheme your sacred name and lift up themselves against you, but all in vain!
Lord, can't you see how I despise those who despise you?
For I grieve when I see them rise up against you.
I have nothing but complete hatred and disgust for them.
Your enemies shall be my enemies!
God, I invite your searching gaze into my heart.
Examine me through and through;
find out everything that may be hidden within me.
Put me to the test and sift through all my anxious cares.
See if there is any path of pain I'm walking on,
and lead me back to your glorious, everlasting way—
the path that brings me back to you.

What do I sense God is trying to show me or say to me in Psalm 139?

_____
_____
_____
_____
_____
_____

Learning Forward

Have I found myself struggling in areas where it's difficult to identify the root cause? What are those areas?

_____
_____
_____
_____

Keep in mind that you might see patterns you've carried from generations before you.

What negative patterns do I notice from past generations? Am I repeating any of these?

___
___
___
___

> I was a great storyteller who could make any story about myself so real that it became my reality… except for the fact that it wasn't true! Because of past wounds, I made up stories and clung to them so tightly that when confronted with the truth, it shattered me. I felt so shocked and shifted, and it would take me weeks to recover and come back into reality.

Do I have stories I've made up about myself that originated in past woundedness and pain? What are they?

___
___
___
___

Breathwork/Meditation

Inhale for a count of 10. Feel all the feels. Allow the chaos to be fully present.

Hold the breath for a count of 11. This is the space where you consider the sound advice you have received or the right thing you know is your next step: What will you choose? This is the shift, where you know you are alone with your choice, yet you are still seen, heard, and held.

Exhale for a count of 12: God says, "Surrender the chaos to Me. Know that I am a God of completion and source. I will bring every resource necessary for your success and the success of those around you as you surrender it to Me."

Journal your thoughts below after doing this exercise.

___
___
___

_____
_____
_____
_____
_____

Declarations and Decrees

- God, my Creator and Heavenly Father, is so aware of me.
- I am known and perceived by the God of the universe.
- Every detail of my life is known intimately by my Heavenly Father, and it is safe to be known by Him.
- I am aware of the intimacy I share with God.
- My future is prepared for me, and I step into it with a bright awareness.
- My life journey leaves a trail of kindness.
- Blessings are imparted to me daily and in all circumstances.
- I am tangibly aware of the wonderful, deep, and incomprehensible love that is heaped onto me from the Father.
- I have childlike wonder, faith, and strength.
- I cannot run or hide; it is impossible for me to disappear from Your presence.
- My days and nights are never dark with God by my side.
- I was formed and shaped with intricacy and delicacy, woven together in my mother's womb.
- I am mysteriously complex and becoming more aware of my wonderful complexities.
- I was created in a secret place, with care and skill.
- From nothing, I was formed into something.
- I am willing to become more aware of me.
- I am willing to become more aware of my Creator.

Write some more of your own declarations and decrees below:

-
-

Tips for writing your own declarations and decrees:
Is it true according to God's Word and how He sees you? Is it present tense?
Compare it to the Word of the Lord for what is true, and since everything that Jesus died to give us is here and now, the decrees need to be present tense.

My goal in helping you acknowledge pain from the past that resulted in your emotional triggers is to practice feeling your feelings without letting them render you unable to function. Feeling peace while peeling back the layers allows you to actually experience the grace to rewrite your own story. It's bringing Jesus into the center of your story where He belongs. The peace and grace of God are more than abundant for the task! You can learn how to go inside yourself at any time and identify if your emotions and self-beliefs are contributing to a false reality. The all-surpassing peace and full freedom of God are yours through the Shift of Awareness.

Below, take as long as you need to journal about past pain that has contributed to emotional triggers and to identify any emotions or self-beliefs that contribute to a false reality.

The Shift of Support

When it comes to Being Supported, you might recognize the need for this shift because of feeling isolated, alone, and disconnected. You notice yourself pushing people and things away. Maybe you've left a relationship in an unhealthy way. Maybe you choose to cause drama in relationships so others will keep you at arm's length or abandon you altogether. Resisting the Shift of Being Supported looks like avoiding vulnerability, sabotaging any possibility of receiving real care from another human.

Like me, maybe you're willing to go to battle for others but won't allow others to fight for you. My warrior spirit always wants to fight…even when it's time to rest. I've come to realize much of the Shift of Being Supported happens while learning to receive from the right people. This helps the battle subside and allows you to surrender into rest and receiving.

All of our trust issues cause the screeching halt of our internal brakes trying to stop this shift. We fear opening up to the support of another because we can't trust how that's going to turn out. We don't want to be disappointed or hurt again. But acknowledging the presence of our difficulty trusting others doesn't threaten God's design of unity and needing the right people in our lives. To be our best, we must be Supported. We also get to learn the value of the support we can give to others too.

Many times, when we are recovering from trauma and growing, newfound self-awareness can feel overwhelming. We may begin to feel stuck, paralyzed, and questioning, "How did I even get here? How did I become this person?" We need a solid support system to remind us of our value and worth during these overwhelming moments. Supportive people help us remember that growth comes in seasons and things will not feel hard forever.

In my healing journey, my natural instinct has been to push away support, because receiving support requires vulnerability. For me, this tendency manifests itself through conflict. Fighting against someone or something helps me feel present and connected to what is going on around me. My default was to purposefully reject support rather than accept it. This is not healthy and has been one of the hardest things for me to work through in my personal journey. I've learned the key to growth is the power of going deep inside yourself instead of fighting against or pushing away that which comes to help you grow.

Do you remember the story of Zacchaeus in the Bible? He climbed a tree to be able to see Jesus. He had to create space for himself to grow, no matter the circumstances or opinions of others. Do you remember the woman with the issue of blood? This woman had to strip away all fears of rejection and judgment to go after her own healing. Just like the healed woman and Zacchaeus, they probably felt extremely uncomfortable when considering their options to chase after change. But they chose to wholeheartedly believe in the bigness of Jesus, and they found the bigness of themselves. They also found themselves surrounded by witnesses to their pivotal moments. We can assume that some of these witnesses then became part of their supportive community. Entering into a vulnerable state with themselves, with people, and with God changed their lives forever.

Allow yourself to be a big, messy grower, and allow others to support you in it.

Ask Questions

How and where can I find the right people for my support system?

_____
_____
_____
_____
_____
_____

Who are the people/who is a person I would like to have in my support system?

_____
_____
_____
_____

Do I recognize their willingness to open up to me? What is one small step I can take to get to know this person/these people better?

_____
_____
_____
_____

What is one small step I can take to allow myself to trust this person/these people more?

_____
_____
_____
_____

Tangible Tools

You've probably heard of making a Vision Board. In similar fashion, let's make a Support Board. Find photos or symbols of the people you know are in your corner cheering for you. Maybe you're not sure who "your people" are yet, and that's okay! Take a few moments to think of *any* form of support you have in your life right now.

What words describe the support I have? What pictures can I find that represent or remind me of them?

_____

_____

_____

_____

If you'd prefer, draw out a Support Board here or create a sketch of what support looks like to you:

The Sounds of His Voice

Psalm 91 (TPT)

*When you abide under the shadow of Shaddai,
you are hidden in the strength of God Most High.
He's the hope that holds me and the stronghold to shelter me,
the only God for me, and my great confidence.
He will rescue you from every hidden trap of the enemy,
and he will protect you from false accusation and any deadly curse.
His massive arms are wrapped around you, protecting you.
You can run under his covering of majesty and hide.
His arms of faithfulness are a shield keeping you from harm.
You will never worry about an attack of demonic forces at night
nor have to fear a spirit of darkness coming against you.
Don't fear a thing!
Whether by night or by day, demonic danger will not trouble you,
nor will the powers of evil be launched against you.
Even in a time of disaster, with thousands and thousands being killed,
you will remain unscathed and unharmed.
You will be a spectator as the wicked perish in judgment,
for they will be paid back for what they have done!
When we live our lives within the shadow of God Most High,
our secret hiding place, we will always be shielded from harm.
How then could evil prevail against us or disease infect us?
God sends angels with special orders to protect you wherever you go,
defending you from all harm.
If you walk into a trap, they'll be there for you and keep you from stumbling.
You'll even walk unharmed among the fiercest powers of darkness,
trampling every one of them beneath your feet!
For here is what the Lord has spoken to me:
"Because you loved me, delighted in me, and have been loyal to my name,
I will greatly protect you.
I will answer your cry for help every time you pray,
and you will feel my presence in your time of trouble.
I will deliver you and bring you honor.
I will satisfy you with a full life and with all that I do for you.
For you will enjoy the fullness of my salvation!*

What do I sense God is trying to show me or say to me in Psalm 91?

_____
_____
_____

_____

_____

_____

_____

Learning Forward

I recall a time at work when I made a big mistake...like HUGE. Many team members supported me and helped fix it, and even though I cried myself to sleep that night, I knew I was supported. Should it have been considered a failure? By most companies, it could have even been a fireable offense, but I learned forward. I grew so much through that experience. I can't consider it a failure now, knowing how I dramatically improved my skills at work, my willingness to allow others to support me, and my trust in myself that I could turn any mistake into a growth moment and learn forward.

What "failures" have I had that have tried to steal my growth opportunity?

_____

_____

_____

_____

How can I reframe one of my failures as being an opportunity for growth and learning instead?

_____

_____

_____

_____

Breathwork/Meditation

Sit outside somewhere in the grass, dirt, or on a rock.

Bring your favorite bottle of high-quality essential oil. (I like dōTerra Anchor, arborvitae, or cedarwood.) Place a few drops of oil into your palm, and then cup your hands over your nose.

Inhale deeply, imagining your breath flowing through every inch of your body. Direct your breath with your intention as the essential oil molecules enter your body at the cellular level. *(I won't try to explain scientifically how this works. I'm not a scientist, doctor, or psychologist...I'm just a girl who has done a lot of healing and has a basic understanding of how essential oils can help us heal.)*

As you continue to take deep breaths, feel the ground beneath you. Notice how solid it is. Try to imagine shifting it - moving it. Notice how it is solid, through and through.

Ask yourself, "Can I trust this ground? Am I willing to let it support me a little more right now?"

On your next full exhale, sink deeper into the support of the earth. As you feel more supported, thank Jesus for His creation. Express gratitude for the stability of the earth and gravity.

Express gratitude toward yourself for allowing support and stability in your life in many ways. Remind yourself that you are perfectly supported in every moment.

As you begin to notice a lightness, as if you may float away, envision going inside yourself and seeing the fullness of who God created you to be. See yourself growing into that fullness.

Journal your thoughts below after completing this breathwork/meditation.

Visualizing

See the closed rose and how it holds beauty yet to be revealed and encapsulates a fullness of aroma yet to be sensed. Now, imagine yourself as the rose. As you release control, you open yourself up. Picture your bigness to start to see the fullness of your beauty come forth. Remind yourself that the rose naturally reveals itself; it safely blooms and fully opens its petals for all to see its center. The truth is, the rose is more beautiful open than closed; the same is for you.

If you are feeling stuck, ask yourself who or what am I hiding from?

_____
_____
_____
_____
_____

What causes me to feel like I need to stay closed?

_____
_____
_____
_____
_____

Why does blooming feel vulnerable to me?

_____
_____
_____
_____
_____

Declarations and Decrees

Declare these things over yourself from Psalm 91:

- I am safe and secure.
- I am supported and protected.
- I decree that it is safe for me to enjoy the fullness (the bigness) of all that my salvation allows me to participate in.
- I decree that I am satisfied with His fullness and never plan to stop pursuing it.
- I decree that as I allow God to wrap me under His covering, I allow His support to solidify the work He has done in me.
- I allow our secret hiding place to take me from glory to glory so He is glorified in my growth.
- I decree that I delight in Him, His ways of doing things, and I allow His people and His creation to support me as I also support them.

Write some more of your own here:

-
-

Below, take as long as you need to journal about what has come up in your heart during this Shift of Being Supported conversation.

The Shift of Perseverance

We need the Shift of Perseverance when we're faced with dreams that seem dead or difficult circumstances. Traveling the road out of my past has been hard. Having hunger and drive to explore your flaws, your gifts, your shortcomings, and your strengths can be an overwhelming challenge. I have learned that this road is not for the faint of heart.

Personally, I don't want to spend any more days in apathy and idleness. I have a hunger to go after the mysteries of God, the truth of His Kingdom, and the love He has for me. The Shift of Perseverance is learning to stay hungry and persistent, not back down, and allow the victorious, virtuous cycle to carry us onward. Perseverance teaches us to love the process of growth and to be filled with heightened awareness. Making the decision to persevere makes it easier. Aligning ourselves with that one decision allows us to flow forward and live a life of #holyshifts even when it looks big and hard.

The most important *why* you'll ever ask is: **why will I persevere?** The answer to this question will keep you going on the hard days. But it may not be as simple to answer as you may think. You have to know the right answer…YOUR right answer. It can't be someone else's reason to keep going. It's not a Sunday school answer or a motivational speaker-of-the-minute mantra. What is big enough to keep you going no matter what? Deep inside, you have to know you matter; what you go through gives you authority and helps you provide breakthroughs for others. Your perseverance is not just for you.

This shift is actually one of the hardest for me to write about. Out of everything you will read in *Own Your Shift,* Perseverance is the thing that feels hardest to shift. I believe the difficulty is because perseverance is not about willpower; it's about surrender. It's about continuously saying yes to the dream inside of you and letting God's grace be enough for each day, each moment. Our surrender means not worrying about tomorrow or even an hour from now.

We may not be able to see what's coming next, but we can still have vision for the road ahead. This is why it is crucial to fall in love with the journey instead of the destination.

If I'm being brutally honest, another word for perseverance is *discipline*. And it appears that God's Word tells us the key to being disciplined and persevering is receiving divine insight about our dreams. So maybe, if you're like me, you aren't always a disciplined person. Especially when obstacles and setbacks come, sometimes my good habits and practices fall by the wayside. But because I've chosen to regularly receive God's divine insight about my dreams, being a person of discipline comes more easily. I want to see His will and purposes fulfilled in my life so much, and therefore, I'm able to persist.

No matter the pain we have experienced, we believe God has a plan for our desires. We persevere by actively saying "yes" to whatever doors God leads us through. Although time may heal all wounds, time is not meant to "heal" or remove our dreams. As we allow our hearts to be mended, we envision our dreams and desires with even greater clarity and zeal. We pursue healing so we can persevere into our destinies!

Ask Questions

Why will I persevere?

_____
_____
_____
_____
_____
_____
_____

Do I criticize myself? Do I punish myself for not being okay or for having a bad day? If so, in what situations or circumstances do I notice this most?

_____
_____
_____
_____
_____

Can I allow myself to truly embrace the days, weeks, years, where everything just seems to suck? Can I freely admit that had things not sucked so badly to this point, I wouldn't be on the journey of Owning My Shift? In what way(s) am I judgmental toward myself about my past?

_____
_____
_____
_____
_____

> Things will get better as you get better.

Will I choose to believe that things will change *as I change?* What things in me do I most want to see change?

_____
_____
_____
_____
_____

Even if many of my life circumstances have been beyond my control, will I allow myself to see that now is *my* time? What would it look like to accept my role as the main character, the star in my life?

_____
_____
_____
_____
_____

Because of Jesus' sacrifice, you deserve to live out the desires of your heart.

Do I struggle with believing that I can live out the desires of my heart or that I deserve to? What are the desires of my heart?

_____
_____
_____
_____
_____

Do I know what it means to relish in the Lord? Do I know how?

_____
_____
_____

Practice using all five of your senses to immensely enjoy God. After you practice this, take a moment to describe how it felt:

_____
_____
_____
_____
_____

Tangible Tools

Sometimes it's hard to acknowledge all of the GOOD around us. Write down some things that bring you joy, love, make you smile, or that you are grateful for:

_____
_____
_____
_____
_____
_____
_____

The Sounds of His Voice

Psalm 37:4 (ESV)

Delight yourself in the Lord, and he will give you the desires of your heart.

James 1:2-4 (TPT)

My fellow believers, when it seems as though you are facing nothing but difficulties, see it as an invaluable opportunity to experience the greatest joy that you can! For you know that when your faith is tested it stirs up in you the power of endurance. And then as your endurance grows even stronger, it will release perfection into every part of your being until there is nothing missing and nothing lacking.

Romans 5:3-5 (TPT)

But that's not all! Even in times of trouble we have a joyful confidence, knowing that our pressures will develop in us patient endurance. And patient endurance will refine our character, and proven character leads us back to hope. And this hope is not a disappointing fantasy, because we can now experience the endless love of God cascading into our hearts through the Holy Spirit who lives in us!

Galatians 6:9 (TPT)

And don't allow yourselves to be weary in planting good seeds, for the season of reaping the wonderful harvest you've planted is coming!

Did one of these verses stand out to me today? If so, why? What do I sense God is trying to show me or say to me in these verses?

_____
_____
_____
_____
_____

Learning Forward

Healing "on-the-go" might be the crucial key to a Perseverance Shift. We understand that for most of us, life is hard. Our hearts and egos get wounded. Our mindsets become cloudy and weary. Even during periods of time when things seem to be going well we encounter bad days for one reason or another. Healing on-the-go keeps those bad days from becoming bad weeks, and then some.

If you had to rate your ability to heal on-the-go, would you say you're a 0 (I have no idea how to help myself when things get really hard), or a 10 (I easily keep moving forward with my eyes on my dream while addressing any heart issues that arise), or somewhere in between? _____

When have I seen myself do well with healing on-the-go?

_____
_____
_____
_____

When have I seen myself get stuck when something got really hard?

_____
_____
_____
_____

Breathwork/Meditation

When you feel trampled on or walked over, imagine breath filling you from your toes to your head. Take a deep breath in and picture the air going up your spine and strengthening you to stand tall and feel supported, knowing God has your back even if no one else does.

Breathing is a tool God provided to show us how He supports us with every inhale and exhale. He gave us an automatic oxygen machine: our respiratory system. Talk about perseverance! We are so supported, we don't even have to think about it.

What are some situations and instances when I can put this breathing tool into practice?

_____
_____
_____
_____
_____

Visualizing

Picture yourself surrounded by a bubble where you are happy and safe.

As you feel the overwhelm from your day, imagine your dream, your goal, the thing you want most inside your bubble with you. It could be a projection on the dome above you or sitting in the bubble with you.

Then, picture yourself grabbing all the overwhelming things and pushing them outside of your bubble.

Next, pick up grace and peace and bring them inside your bubble.

Feel grace and peace surround you as you have released the heaviness, which will help you persevere a little longer. Relish in the lightness.

Describe what happened when you did this visualization:

_____
_____
_____
_____
_____

Show the things that can stay in your bubble and the things that cannot:

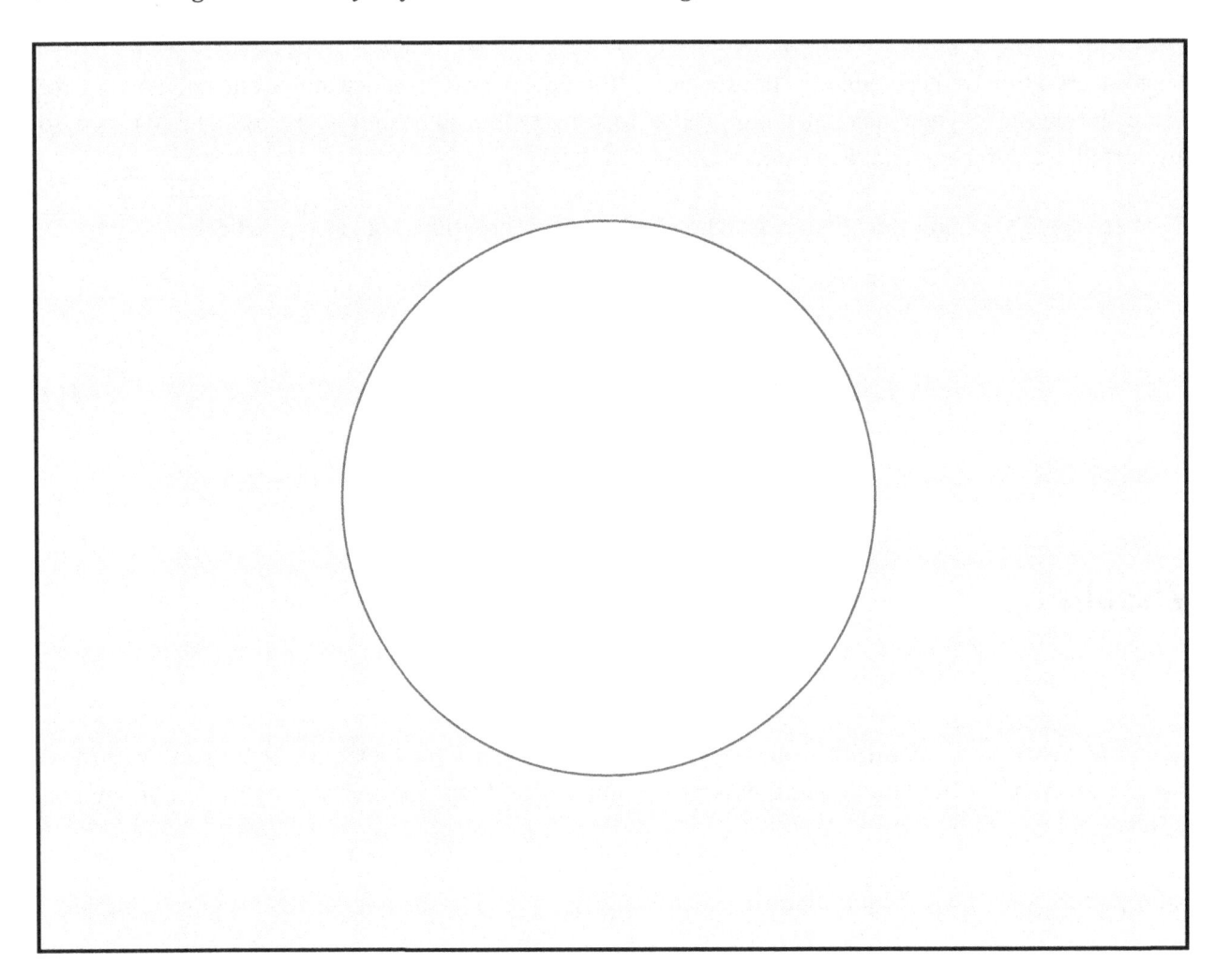

Declarations and Decrees

- True happiness comes as I persevere.
- I can do hard things with joy.
- I am fearfully made and fashioned by the Creator of the universe.
- He has given me purpose, and it's tangibly woven into my DNA as a human. He wants me to have the revelation of who I am.
- I easily discover who I am, what my desires are, and how to function in my purpose.
- I know how to sow good seed into good soil.
- My seed comes back 30-, 60-, and even 100-fold because I persevere to see the harvest.

Write some more of your own here:

-
-

Below, take as long as you need to journal about the Shift of Perseverance, why you will persevere, and the areas in your life where you need this shift.

The Shift of Gratitude

It's time for the Shift of Gratitude. Goodness, this shift has been a hard one for me! I feel like I have a tendency to complain, but I know negativity is not built into the DNA God gave each of us. He gave us joy and a cheerful heart. But just as with any gift we're given, we must choose to take it. We must *choose* joy. The Shift of Gratitude nurtures joy in our lives.

Often, we hear people name things for which they are thankful. If you're like me, you've probably thought expressing gratitude for things many of us simply take for granted (e.g., food, shelter, breath, waking up, etc.) is just "lip service." But, because the power of life and death is in the tongue (Proverbs 18:21), our words do matter. If negative words can cause roots of negativity to grow, our "lip service" can actually serve to establish a root of joy in our lives instead. Gratitude could be seen as a skill that requires practice. With practice, we move from a flippant, "Thanks, God for…," to having a heart filled with thanksgiving and overflowing with joy that bursts forth at every opportunity.

Expressing gratitude is a tangible action that establishes the fruit of joy in our lives. We have been given even more joy than we can take, but often we allow our past terrors, fear, and trauma to justify why we are cranky, sad, or mad. But the good news is, we no longer have to settle for or be slaves to *the poverty of joy*. When we know better, we can do better. And now we know we can choose gratitude as a doorway to joy long before we ever "feel happy."

A few years back, I started something in our family called "Thankful and Prayers." We do it every night as a family. I needed to be reminded every night that there was something good in our lives, and we could, in fact, be grateful. I was hurting so badly that I used my family to help heal me. My intentions may not have been pure, but God took that time and redeemed it. I will not cease to mention Romans 8:28, because it is true. God does work all things together for our good when we love Him. He turned my broken places into healed places.

After a year or so, I could see the fruit coming from our time as a family being grateful. We went from a begrudging "thankful" and an obligatory "prayer" to a whole host of thankfuls and a happy rotation of who prayed that night. Many years in, this has become a favored routine in our home. Even if we're not together because of travel or work, we call each other to participate.

Joy can come in a variety of ways, but I believe gratitude is the key to unlocking that door. Gratitude is a state of our hearts, and our hearts must be aligned by gratitude to reveal the fullness of who we are meant to be on earth. And don't worry, we can make the shift of gratitude while still hurting and healing. A willingness to be filled with thanksgiving will uplift you and elevate you to see that God is working all things out for your good. Without gratitude, we remain focused on the mistakes, mishaps, and others' malicious acts in our lives. With gratitude, the good of God always belongs to you. Even the mistakes are learning opportunities, the mishaps are God's providence, and the harm from others becomes miraculous moments of healing we can pass along to anyone who's shared our pain.

Ask Questions

Can I recognize what is already good in my life and do I appreciate what I already have? What are some of the good things?

_____
_____
_____
_____
_____

How do I steward what is already good in my life? Where is there an opportunity for me to become a better steward of the good things in my life?

_____
_____
_____
_____
_____

Do I feel like struggling makes me feel important, therefore I continue to allow the struggle to be present? Why might this be?

_____
_____
_____
_____
_____

Do I feel the need to overcome hard things to prove my worth or value or to become my own hero? Where does this need come from?

_____
_____
_____
_____
_____

Am I indifferent or ungrateful? How aware have I been about the good in my life?

_____
_____
_____

What are some ways I can increase gratitude in my attitude?

_____
_____
_____
_____
_____

Have I always had a generally ungrateful disposition? Was I raised by grateful or ungrateful people? How can I become more grateful?

_____
_____
_____
_____
_____

How can I encourage myself daily to be grateful, no matter what is going on in my life?

_____
_____
_____
_____

Tangible Tools

For my family, we have a nightly routine of verbally processing and taking account of all that is good and right in our lives. Here are the questions we answer, and then we rotate who prays each night.

1. What are you thankful for?
2. What are you proud of yourself for today?
3. What emotion are you thankful for?
4. What is your goal for tomorrow?

Answer those four questions for yourself today:

1. _____
2. _____
3. _____
4. _____

The Sounds of His Voice

Isaiah 61:3

...to bestow on them a crown of beauty instead of ashes,
the oil of joy instead of mourning,
and a garment of praise instead of a spirit of despair.
They will be called oaks of righteousness,
a planting of the Lord for the display of his splendor.

Isaiah 61:7

Instead of your shame you will receive a double portion,
and instead of disgrace you will rejoice in your inheritance.
And so you will inherit a double portion in your land,
and everlasting joy will be yours.

Matthew 14:15- 21 (TPT)

Later that afternoon the disciples came to Jesus and said, "It's going to be dark soon and the people are hungry, but there's nothing to eat here in this desolate place. You should send the crowds away to the nearby villages to buy themselves some food." "They don't need to leave," Jesus responded. "You can give them something to eat." They answered, "But all we have is five barley loaves and two fish." "Let me have them," Jesus replied. Then he had everyone sit down on the grass as he took the five loaves and two fish. He looked up into heaven, gave thanks to God, and broke the bread into pieces. He then gave it to his disciples, who in turn gave it to the crowds. And everyone ate until they were satisfied, for the food was multiplied in front of their eyes! They picked up the leftovers and filled up twelve baskets full! There were about five thousand men who were fed, in addition to many women and children!

Did one of these verses stand out to me today? If so, why? What do I sense God is trying to show me or say to me in these verses?

_____
_____
_____
_____
_____

Learning Forward

Can we agree that it is time to find our voice, the voice that gives thanks to God? Let's also agree that it's time to start discovering what God fully intended for us to experience in life, because as we do, we come alive in the exact way God wants us to. As we come alive, as we find our voice, we get to walk in freedom and help others do the same. I started finding my voice when I became grateful for everything around me and when I turned my eyes and heart towards Him and His goodness.

From Isaiah 61:7: *Instead of your shame you will receive a double portion, and instead of disgrace you will rejoice in your inheritance.*

What "instead of" do I think God is waiting to give me with my thanksgiving?

_____
_____
_____
_____

Breathwork/Meditation/Visualizing

Imagine what it would be like to be on the hillside with Jesus and the disciples as Jesus gives thanks for the fish and loaves, breaks them, and multiplies them.

Close your eyes, take in a deep inhale, filling all of your lungs. Then, a full exhale completely emptying your lungs. Now, repeat that two more times. After your third large exhale, start breathing intentionally, focusing on the air coming in through your nose and leaving through your nose. In and out, in and out... With your eyes still closed and your breath focused, intentional, and slow, try to clear your mind, and slowly let each piece of the image on the hillside come into focus. Imagine the landscape, the hill...was it grassy? Are you sitting or standing? Now, notice the weather. Does it feel warm or cool? Is there a breeze from the water? Now, slowly start to see the disciples. What's it like with them there? Take it in for a moment. Start to fill the landscape with people; the Bible tells us there were 5,000 men, and historians say that women and children were also present. What does the sea of people look like? Sound like? Smell like? Sit with that for a moment. Now, with all of the clarity that you can, bring Jesus into the picture. How does it feel? What do you notice? What does His voice sound like when He gives thanks to God? What does His face look like when He looks up to the heavens? Be there for a minute.

Now, imagine and feel what it's like to help carry a basket and pass out fish and loaves. Are people grateful? Are the kids grabbing at the baskets? Now, what does it feel like to have everyone fed and satisfied and still look over to see full baskets of leftovers? Then, spend some time praising God for all that He did in that scenario. Thank Him that He is still willing to do miracles like that today.

Next, flip the order of the scene. Do your breathing, and all the same steps to prep yourself to go into the vision. But this time, before anything else, imagine Jesus first. Then, add in the details one by one. Do you notice a difference with Jesus being there first? Maybe yes, and maybe no. Every person will experience this exercise completely differently and unique to them. I want you to try this second exercise not for you to feel like you did it wrong the first time, but for you to experience that seeing Jesus first is always the answer. He is everywhere and wants to be with you in all things. He will make every situation fresh, alive, abundant, and *full*.

When you need to remember gratitude, put Him first. You will find that your heart softens more easily, and you feel the person of Jesus to come a little more alive on the inside of you. He is always fully alive, but we can feel distant from Him. He is closer than ever; we just need to come online with Him through gratitude.

Take a moment to describe how this felt or write down anything of note.

_____
_____
_____
_____
_____
_____

Declarations and Decrees

- I am willing to be thankful in all that I do and say.
- My gratitude changes situations.
- I allow God to shift my negativity to an "instead of" through my thanksgiving.
- I am always looking for an opportunity to be grateful.
- Gratitude opportunities seek me out so that I can receive the abundance on the other side.
- I am thankful for my crown of beauty.
- I am thankful for the oil of joy.
- I am thankful for the garment of praise.
- I am thankful to be called an oak of righteousness.
- I am thankful to be a planting of the Lord for the display of His splendor.
- I am thankful for the double portion that God has for me.
- I am thankful for my inheritance and that I have access to it *now*.
- I am thankful for my expanding, double portion of land available to me *now*.
- I am thankful for the everlasting joy that is mine *now*.
- I am thankful for modern-day miracles.
- I am thankful that I can simply look up and say, "Thanks, God," no matter the situation or circumstance.
- Gratitude is my gift.
- My gift of gratitude is for me and everyone around me.
- Negative thinking has no place in my life; it's not from Heaven, so it is not my inheritance.

Write some more of your own here:

-
-

Below, take as long as you need to journal about the areas where you feel the Lord is inviting you into an upgrade. Often, these are the things that feel "hard" or "stuck," so what is He telling you about those areas? Who is He inviting you to become in the process of this upgrade opportunity? What will it feel like on the other side when the upgrade has been made? Who will you get to show up as?

The Shift of Self

The Shift of Self is about you learning to love yourself. How you see yourself, what you believe about yourself, and how you view your relationship with God and others can all shift into love. Just because something terrible happened to us in the past does not entitle us to treat ourselves badly indefinitely. We are far more valuable than the bad we've been through or are going through or may encounter in the future.

There is a power in falling in love with yourself and seeing yourself as intrinsically valuable simply because you are alive! You could have been born at any time, in any place, but you are HERE NOW holding value for this time and place. Loving yourself means believing in your purpose for this very moment. Without loving yourself, you'll never acknowledge the depth and significance you have as a cherished creation.

The first steps of self-love may seem tricky, even controversial. Self-love doesn't mean being selfish…but sometimes it does. It doesn't mean being self-involved…but sometimes it does. As you grow, you will go through seasons of feeling like everything is "all about me," but that's necessary at times. You are healing. You are being selective in how you expend your energy, knowing that giving it *all* away to others hinders your healing process. However, you will notice that as you heal and shift into self-love, loving yourself will effortlessly begin to spill over to others. You may also be asking, "Why are we doing this? This is painful…" Well, we need to work through some of the pain, bring it under the cross, work through forgiving on all fronts in order to get to a place where we can truly start to peel back the layers, become undone in His presence, and reestablish who He made us to be.

I remember the first time I consciously chose to go deep inside of *who* God created me to be. It was painful. It took intention. I was scared of what I would find. but I fell so in love with who I discovered myself to be. My starting point was with everything people had told me was "wrong" about me - "You're too much, too loud, too aggressive," etc.

Let me give you some examples. First, I've been on a health journey. Previously, it has been hard to believe that good health was for me. I've looked in the mirror and told myself I'm disgusting; even as I write this, I am considered "morbidly obese." But are those my words of self-hatred, or did they come from someone else? Perhaps many voices, including mine, have fueled a nasty and shame-filled inner voice. I have fought hard for the revelation of my beauty. Layers and layers of self-awareness have been uncovered.

Also, before I began to love myself, being seen and known by people scared the daylights outta me. I once had a co-worker who walked by and blurted out, "What happened to Happy Holli?" I was in such a dark place in my life, and she saw me. I didn't even know her that well, but she knew who I was created to be: full of joy and happiness. I wasn't actively cultivating joy and happiness in my life. She felt it and was brave enough to call me out. She saw me.

Lastly, pain and anguish lived inside of me for 15 years after I was raped; not a day went by that I didn't think about it. Victim mentality, anxiety, darkness, and fear of what people are capable of plagued me. Constant terror swelled over me like the gloomiest cloud. Panic attacks were a regular occurrence. Satan will try to cover truth with lies. He piles "crap" on top of the true beauty, but our true value is intrinsic and will never tarnish or go away; it is sacred and built into our DNA.

Looking back, I feel like I am unrecognizable from the woman I was in those situations. I am so thankful for that version of myself, for her boldness to keep going and to keep a flicker of hope alive in her heart for something better, something more. I want to encourage you that no matter how painful the experience was or still is, there is hope. You can keep the dreams alive inside of your heart. God-given desires are yours; He gave them to you. Our God is a promise-fulfilling God. And when He makes promises, He provides. It's time to gently unwind the past to be fully in the present.

Ask Questions

What uncomfortable feelings do I experience regularly, no matter how small or trivial they may seem?

_____
_____
_____
_____
_____

Do I tend to brush past my negative feelings quickly or try to cover them up? Do I easily place other things or people over my emotions? Why do I do this?

_____
_____
_____
_____
_____

Does my inner voice say hurtful things to myself in my own head? Have I repeated to myself terrible things others have said to me? What are some of those things?

_____
_____
_____
_____
_____

What negative things have people told me or spoken over me? What are the expectations from my family, friends, and culture that influence my self-talk?

_____
_____
_____
_____
_____

What is the relationship between my love for myself and my love for God?

_____
_____
_____
_____
_____

Does what I believe in my head about self-love and the love of God match what's happening in my heart, emotions, words, and actions? If not, what is incongruent right now?

_____
_____
_____
_____
_____

Do I trust God's ability to have created me? Do I believe He wove my desires into me? Do I believe He is a good Father and wants to help bring those desires into existence? How can I partner with God to bring the desires He placed in me into existence?

_____
_____
_____
_____
_____

If I acknowledge that my gifts and desires can benefit my life but also the lives of those around me, does believing this change my desires or intensify them at all? Why?

_____
_____
_____
_____
_____

When I look at my life, where can I see examples of my desires and dreams popping up but me sabotaging or shutting them down?

_____
_____
_____
_____
_____

How can I rekindle those desires? How can I start to see them become reality?

_____
_____
_____
_____
_____

Tangible Tools

Develop a self-care ritual, spend some time with a furry friend, or go on a laugh quest!

Whether it's taking a bath, giving yourself a manicure or facial, stretching or taking a walk, cooking yourself a healthy meal, etc. (the possibilities are endless), think of things you can do to enjoy a time of stillness between just you and God. What will you do and when?

_____
_____
_____
_____
_____

You could even go on a hunt for funny memes and silly things on the internet to make you smile; save them for later to help you on a bad day.

The Sounds of His Voice

Ephesians 5:29 (TPT)
No one abuses his own body, but pampers it—serving and satisfying its needs. That's exactly what Christ does for his church!

Proverbs 19:8 (TPT)
Do yourself a favor and love wisdom. Learn all you can, then watch your life flourish and prosper!

Mark 12:31
And the second is this: 'You must love your neighbor in the same way you love yourself.' You will never find a greater commandment than these."

2 Timothy 3:1-2 (TPT)
But you need to be aware that in the final days the culture of society will become extremely fierce. People will be self-centered lovers of themselves and obsessed with money. They will boast of great things as they strut around in their arrogant pride and mock all that is right. They will ignore their own families. They will be ungrateful and ungodly.

Psalm 84 (TPT)

For the Pure and Shining One
A prophetic song written by the prophetic singers of Korah's clan
Set to the melody of "For the Feast of Harvest"

God of Heaven's Armies, you find so much beauty in your people!
They're like lovely sanctuaries of your presence.
Deep within me are these lovesick longings, desires and daydreams of living in union with you.
When I'm near you, my heart and my soul will sing and worship with my joyful songs of you, my true source and spring of life!
O Lord of Heaven's Armies, my King and my God, even the sparrows and swallows are welcome to build a nest among your altars to raise their young.
What pleasure fills those who live every day in your temple, enjoying you as they worship in your presence!
Pause in his presence
How enriched are they who find their strength in the Lord; within their hearts are the highways of holiness!
Even when their paths wind through the dark valley of tears, they dig deep to find a pleasant pool where others find only pain.
He gives to them a brook of blessing filled from the rain of an outpouring.
They grow stronger and stronger with every step forward, and the God of all gods will appear before them in Zion.
Hear my cry, O God of Heaven's Armies!
God of Jacob, listen to my loving prayer.
Pause in his presence
God, your wraparound presence is our defense.
In your kindness look upon the faces of your anointed ones.
For just one day of intimacy with you is like a thousand days of joy rolled into one!
I'd rather stand at the threshold in front of the Gate Beautiful, ready to go in and worship my God, than to live my life without you in the most beautiful palace of the wicked.
For the Lord God is brighter than the brilliance of a sunrise!
Wrapping himself around me like a shield, he is so generous with his gifts of grace and glory.
Those who walk along his paths with integrity will never lack one thing they need, for he provides it all!
O Lord of Heaven's Armies, what euphoria fills those who forever trust in you!

Did one of these verses stand out to me today? If so, why? What do I sense God is trying to show me or say to me in these verses?

_____
_____
_____
_____
_____
_____
_____
_____

Learning Forward

We need you. We need your story. You are meant to bring freedom to others. There are people waiting for you to come out of hiding, get off the sidelines, and walk freely in who you were created to be. Just as I am being seen by you through this book, you can know it is safe to step out, begin your healing journey, and be seen. I hope you see yourself in my stories of learning to love myself. As you learn to love yourself and step into your authentic truth, you will begin to help others step into theirs. You can share your stories, your wisdom, and your tools. What you have is valuable.

You have a voice for a reason. You have lived your life for a reason. It's time to combine the two: your voice and your life. You can take the mess you lived through and create a message. And you don't have to have it all figured out yet. I am still a work in progress and will never proclaim to be anything else. I simply keep using these tools, day-by-day, moment-by-moment.

What are the stories you need to tell that will bring breakthrough to others?

_____
_____
_____
_____
_____
_____

What are the words and the things keeping you on the sideline? Draw or write what is possible when you step onto the field:

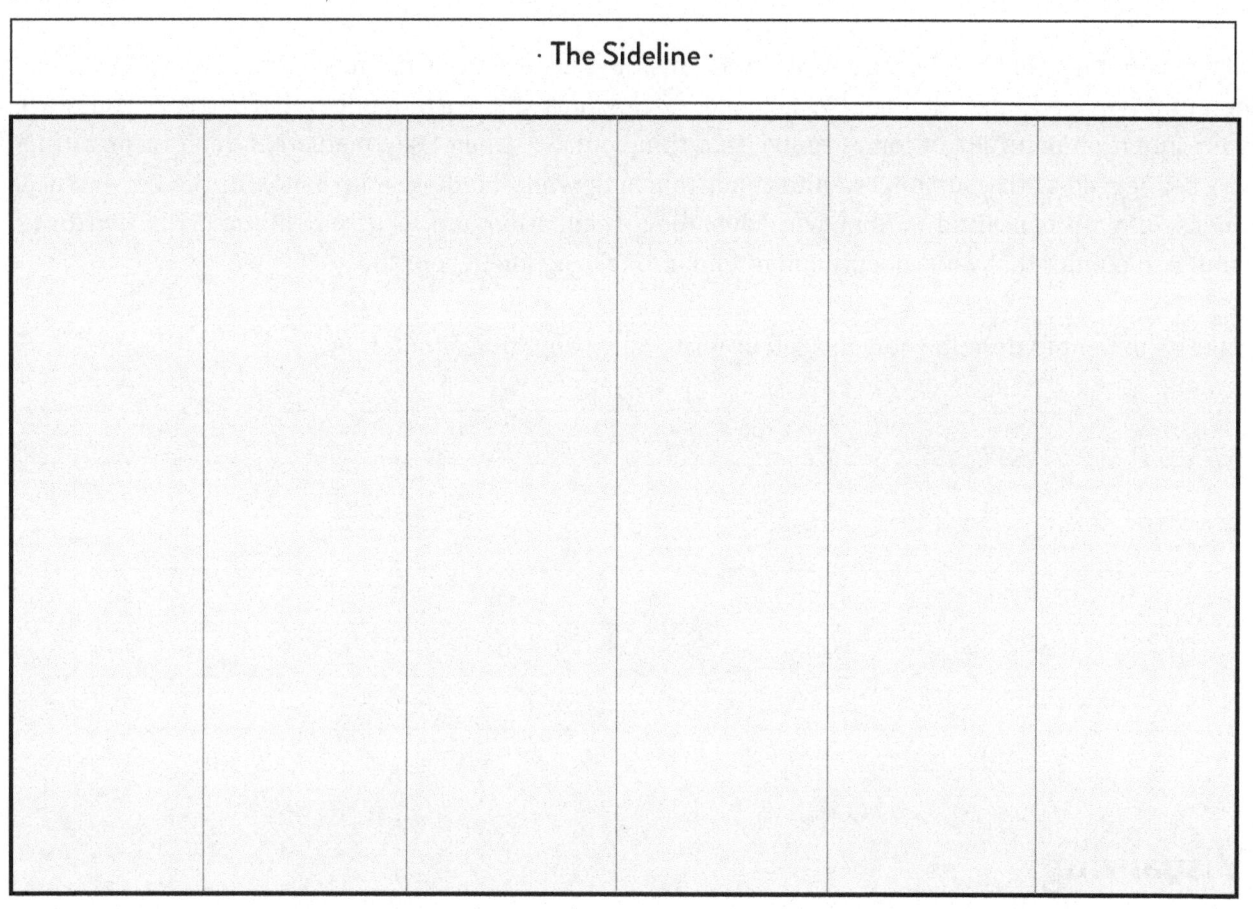

· The Sideline ·

The field of life is always bigger; it's where the action happens! Don't stay on the sidelines; it's small, and we were never meant to live there.

Breathwork/Meditation

Meditate on the verses I shared for this shift. Find portions that feel right for you in each season of your life. Here's an example:

Psalm 84:6 (TPT): *Even when their paths wind through the dark valley of tears, they dig deep to find a pleasant pool where others find only pain. He gives to them a brook of blessing filled from the rain of an outpouring.*

Repeat the words inside yourself a few times. Focus on breathing the words in, and exhaling words out. Tune into the most impactful words and phrases. Use your will to align personal intention with God's heart for you through His Word. Allow the verse that you pick to become part of you, alive and active like Hebrews 4:12 states it is. Allow Holy Spirit to breathe on the verse to help it come alive.

There is not a "right" or "wrong" way to do this; just keep Him at the forefront always. One of the definitions of meditate is *to intend.* When you practice and explore a thought until it becomes your own, your intention naturally becomes to live that thing out. So, when I say mediate, I don't mean sitting crossed-legged with your finger and thumb touching while holding your hands in the air. Instead, release any preconceived notions you have about meditation and focus on Him and His Word. It's simple to ponder that verse deeply and intend it to take action in your life.

Take a moment to describe how this felt or write down anything of note:
_____
_____
_____
_____
_____
_____
_____
_____

Visualizing

Knowing you are a masterpiece is one of the most important visions I need you to catch. When you can see clearly the masterpiece you are, life feels a little...well, *a lot* easier. Living life as a masterpiece is more manageable, more engaging, and more enjoyable.

Please take the next few minutes to be seated on the ground or in a chair with your feet firmly planted. Feel yourself grounded and supported...

Close your eyes and start to drift off into a whimsical world of ease and grace where you show up and things are always working for your good. There is always enough abundance to go around; all of your needs and wants are met. There is laughter and joy that saturates the air.

Hang there for a moment. Feel the lightness...this is what it feels like to love living in your own body. The more you practice getting in touch with your Creator and the masterful creation that you are, the more light, easy, beautiful, joy-filled, and just downright phenomenal your life will feel and be. Living here can be possible with practice, intention, and co-creation with God.

Be willing to come back to this place of lightness and envision it over and over until your Creator reveals your path to experience truly knowing yourself, loving yourself, honoring yourself, and living in full alignment and congruence with who your Creator designed and fashioned you to be.

After you try this, take a moment to describe what happened during the experience.

_____
_____
_____
_____
_____
_____

Declarations and Decrees

- I know my life can be lived in vibrant color where all promises come to be.
- I will celebrate my dedication and success.
- I will passionately show up for myself daily, moment by moment.
- I will let God be the leading and guiding light.
- I will step out and challenge myself in new ways.
- I will learn; I will be teachable and fluid to what He is doing.
- I will stay dedicated to what He is doing and continue to say *yes* to all that He has for me.
- I am a target of Heaven.
- I open myself to all of the abundance that's already mine.
- Daily, I allow myself to be known and loved by my Creator.
- I emanate love for my Savior, for myself, and for my neighbors.
- Love flows out of me with ease.
- I will grow into all of the potential that God fashioned within me.
- I will continue to shed all that is holding me back.
- All that is heavy, I release.

Write some more of your own here:

-
-

Below, take as long as you need to journal about your value and the fact that God created you as a unique individual; there never has been and never will be another *you* on the planet.

The Shift of Obedience

This is the Shift of Obedience. Can you imagine what it would be like to always say *yes* to every opportunity in your life and know you would never experience a poor outcome? Many of us are great at people-pleasing and have felt the burden of wanting to say *no* more often. And because many of us are familiar with living in fear of taking risks, even risks that could improve our lives, saying *no* to ourselves comes easy. As hard as it might be to believe, God wants our unconditional *yes* because He only offers us opportunities with positive outcomes. But before we can truly see His kindness and goodness, we have to shift into obedience, obeying the choices He makes available to us.

Our Creator is the only One worthy of requesting our unconditional obedience. Because He put our desires in our DNA, we can trust Him to place us on the path toward the fulfillment of every one of those desires as He intends. Our *yes* to Him determines our course, our health, our happiness, and our influence on the world around us.

There are a few significant times in my life that I can deem "life-changing events." Things like marrying my husband, saying yes to Jesus, having our son Micah; all those are choices I planned and made. But some life-changing events were moments of straight obedience – things I didn't intend to do or have a desire for but had a still, small voice request of me. These moments often feel bigger than me. I may not understand them, but they take me on journeys of which I cannot possibly anticipate the outcome. God asked me to do something, and I had to simply respond with *yes* or *no*.

One of these moments of obedience required my *yes* before the question was asked. God must have known it would be a hard *yes* for me. In March 2019, I was having some quiet time journaling and listening to worship music as I do most mornings. While listening to the Lord, I heard a nudge.

"Will you say *yes* to Me?"

"Of course, Lord. What is it?"

That conversation with God led to a conversation about a job opportunity with the 100X team. Although I was not looking for a job, this was the *yes* He was looking for. As I write this, I just celebrated three years of serving 100X and Pedro as he leads the movement. Obedience is one of the greatest gifts that He could have given me. I have grown tremendously. I have seen brokenness, orphan tendencies, heart wounds, mental blocks, spiritual gaps, my relationships, and my finances all drastically improved because of a simple act of obedience.

Simple obedience might not come easy to some because of past wounds; wounds can taint our willingness. You may have scars from painful experiences; I did too. But please know that an encounter with simple obedience is available to you too. The encounter with your Creator, the opportunity to say *yes* to the goodness He has for you, and to experience His kindness. The chance to change your life, your family's lives, and to leave the legacy that's in your heart to leave.

I know you. I know you don't want to be broken. I know that you don't want to carry around baggage. I know that you don't want to leave it for your loved ones to deal with either. I know you are strong, because you were hurt and are still here pressing in for what's next, willing to heal and learn. I know pain has changed you and helped you build walls to keep you "safe," but I want to encourage you that in a place of safety, you can surrender to the One who cares most for your heart; the One who created your heart. You can lean in with confidence when He asks you to take a bold step because you were willing to trust Him.

On the journey, you will learn His intention for you is incredible and that your wounds will heal along the way. You just need to be willing to go, willing to change on the journey, willing to sever ties to things that weigh you down and keep you bound in hurt, pain, fear, and disobedience.

Ask Questions

Am I ready and willing to say *yes* to God and His plans even when it feels hard and uncomfortable? Are there any areas of my life where obedience seems more difficult? What are they?

_____

_____

_____

_____

Can I recognize how disobedience keeps me stuck and perpetuates blaming myself, God, and others for my life situations and unhappiness?

_____

_____

Am I willing to surrender my desires to God, knowing He gave them to me? What are the desires and dreams that I need to surrender to God?

_____

_____

_____

_____

> God speaks differently in different seasons.

Am I willing to shift and change my ability to hear Him in the different seasons so I can say *yes* when He asks? In my mind, when God speaks to me, what do I "expect" that it will be like/sound like/look like?

_____
_____
_____
_____
_____

> When things don't work out how we thought they would, it is often one of two things: either we deliberately disobeyed, or God has something much better for us.

Are there areas in my life that I hold a grudge against God because it didn't turn out like I wanted? What are those areas? Will I choose to forgive God?

_____
_____
_____
_____
_____

Will I exchange my ideas for His ideas, knowing they are always better for me, because He is a good and kind Dad who wants the absolute best for me? What ideas do I need to exchange?

_____
_____
_____
_____
_____

Am I willing to say yes to the area of upgrade He is inviting me into on the other side of my obedience?

_____
_____
_____

Tangible Tools

Have you read the parable of Jenny and the Pearl Necklace? The author and origin of the story are unknown, but this story was always the inspiration behind my willingness to say *yes* to God. I know He will never make me a bad offer; I have to just get my heart in check. Here is a quick summary, but please take a moment to find the full story on the internet and read through it.

A young girl named Jenny wanted her very own $2 dime store pearl necklace and worked extra chores to earn and buy one. It was her prized possession, and she wore them every day. One night, her loving father asked Jenny if she loved him, and then asked her to give him the pearls. She was unwilling to give them to him after several of his requests. After feeling conviction and sadness, she finally offered her pearls to her father, who, in return, gifted her a blue velvet box of genuine pearls he had been ready to give her all along. What if you could practice the moral of the story? Not only can we be on the receiving side of God's goodness when we say *yes* to Him, but we can help others receive as well.

Think of someone in your life who you can bless. You might not have to ask them for their *yes*, but maybe you can upgrade their life in one way or another. Maybe you are in financial abundance and could support a family vacation for someone who really needs it. Maybe you can buy a coffee for someone to lift their day. Or maybe you'd perform some other act of service or kindness.

Take a few minutes and ask God how you can step out to be the "pearl-necklace-giver" and what that would look like to help upgrade someone's day. Who would it be? How would you do it? When you do this, don't be surprised when God blesses you back. It's amazing...the cycle of #holyshift moments that can come from one act of obedience.

_____
_____
_____
_____

The Sounds of His Voice

Jeremiah 29:11

"For I know the plans I have for you," declares the Lord, "plans to prosper you and not to harm you, plans to give you hope and a future."

What do I sense God is trying to show me or say to me in Jeremiah 29:11?

_____
_____
_____
_____
_____
_____

Learning Forward

His Voice is always there – our ears just need to tune in.

1. His Voice is often subtle. Most of the time, it sounds like saying your name inside your head. Have I ever heard His voice? When? What did He say?

   _____
   _____
   _____

2. His scriptures are alive, active, and ready to help you out of the darkest of times. Have I ever had a verse come alive to my spirit when I read it? Which one?

   _____

3. When you know His Voice and you know His Word through Scripture, you are able to walk in obedience with a full and grateful heart, even if you do not understand the difficult times you're facing. What could I do to grow in confidence regarding His voice and Word?

   _____
   _____
   _____

4. Knowing His Voice will give you the opportunity to say *yes* to Him, even when things don't make sense to you. Has He ever asked me for my yes? When? _____

5. Jeremiah 29:11 shows us God is a good Dad and He has good plans for us. This scripture reminds me that when He asks me to do something, He never intends to harm me. I can always say *yes* to Him because He always wants good for me. Do I trust that God has only good plans for me?
   _____

6. He wants to prosper us. He will lead us into situations of which prosperity and goodness are the outcomes. What situations has He led me to that have been good and prosperous?
   _____
   _____
   _____

7. What He is willing to do for one, He is willing to do for another. What have I seen God do in the lives of others?
   _____
   _____
   _____
   _____

   Am I confident He will do it for me too? _____

I hope you can start to see how safe it is to say *yes* to Him – how safe it is to step out when He is asking you to. Learning to hear and respond to the sound of His voice is so worth it!

Breathwork/Meditation

Let's do a very simple exercise to practice saying *yes* to God.

Close your eyes.

Cycle through slow and steady continuous breathing: in through the nose, out through the mouth. On the exhale through the mouth, I want you to practice verbally saying *yes* with your breath. It might feel or sound weird at first, but a little practice never hurt anyone. Open your heart to your Heavenly Father and let Him know this *yes* is for Him and you are softening your heart to say *yes* to Him.

So that the speed of your obedience is quick, continue practicing this whenever you can. Open your heart to Him, intentionally breathe in and out, and let your breath be your *yes*. With every breath of your life, may it be a *yes* to Him; may your *yes* bring prosperity and hope to your future. I pray that your *yes* satisfies the longing and desires in your heart through Him and that it would all give Him glory.

What happened during this breathwork meditation exercise?

_____
_____
_____
_____
_____
_____
_____

Visualizing

We all have desires. Even if you're not aware of all of them, you have desires inside of you. Your DNA has promises and desires built in from God. It's time to practice seeing those desires come to life. God will ask you to interact with those desires, and it might look like giving them to Him before He allows them to manifest in your life. This visualization will be an exercise you can come back to again and again.

Grab some coloring tools (markers, paints, pens, pencils, etc.). Below, sketch one desire that's in your heart - something you have longed for, wanted, or thought about for a long time. Maybe you've shared it with others, maybe not. But this drawing is just for you and God. Take a few minutes to complete your drawing, and don't worry about your artistic ability (or lack thereof). Also, there is no desire that is "wrong." This is your heart, your life, your will; you get to choose.

Is it a new house? Putting a water well in Africa? A family vacation? Launching a business? Having multiple commas in your bank account? You pick. Then, sketch it.

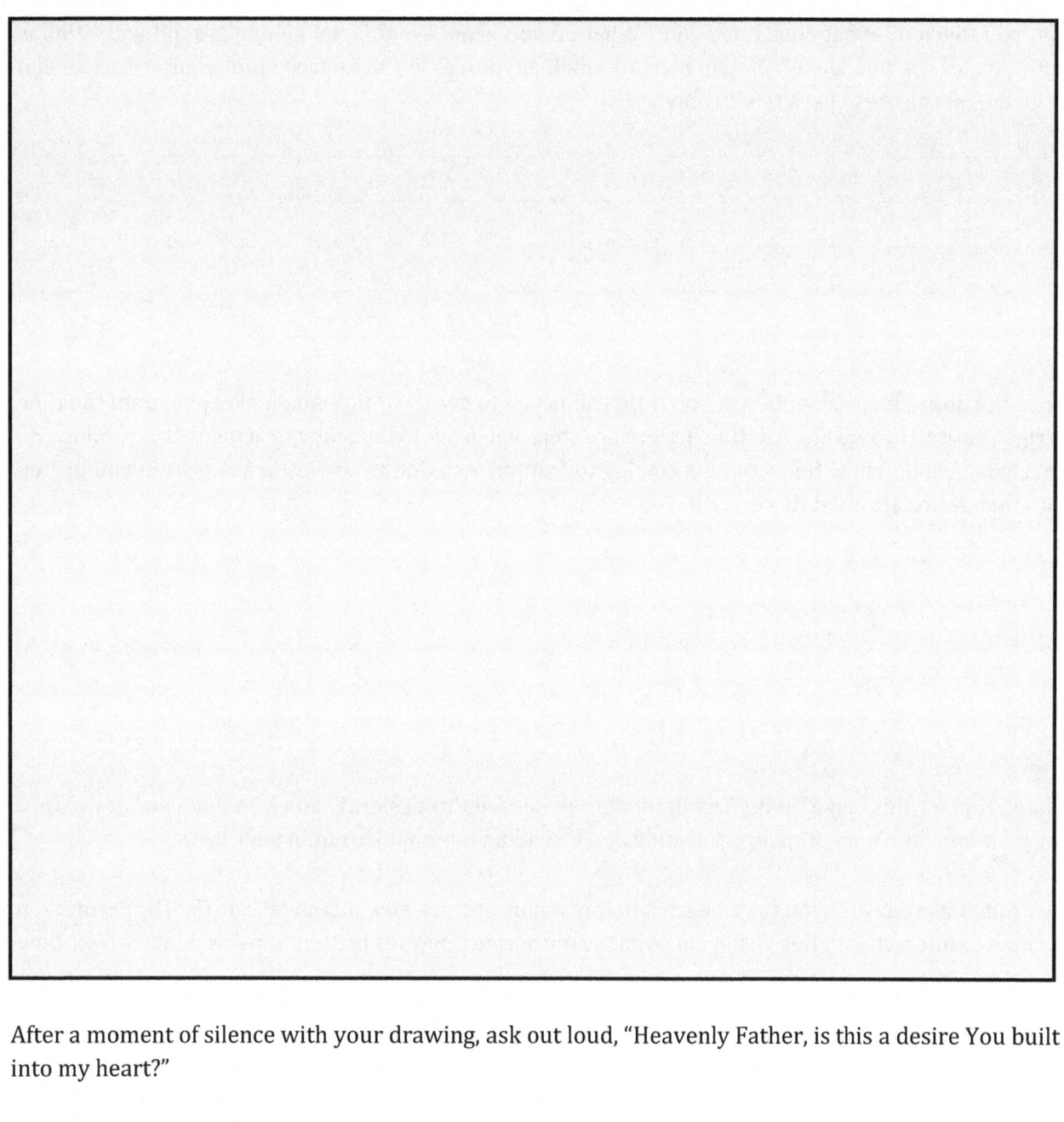

After a moment of silence with your drawing, ask out loud, "Heavenly Father, is this a desire You built into my heart?"

What does God want to tell you about that desire? He will probably say, "Yes," because our desires have a purpose for us. But there may be more He wants to share with you about the desire to help you better understand yourself. If you're not sensing a *yes* from God, ask Him if there is something else He wants you to focus on in this season of your life.

Once you have approval from Him that it *is* a desire He gave you, close your eyes and imagine the desire fulfilled in the present time.

Can you touch it? What does it feel like? What do you hear? What is happening around you? Who is with you, or are you alone? Do you taste or smell anything? Try to engage all of your senses as you envision this desire being a reality now.

_____
_____
_____
_____
_____

Once the desire feels tangible, ask God if He wants you to give it to Him for safekeeping until the time is right for it to be real life. Ask Him if there are steps you need to take now to activate this promise He gave you. Ask God how He pictures it coming to fruition. Ask God what *yes* He needs from you to step into that desire. How did He respond?

_____
_____
_____
_____
_____

Thank Him for this opportunity. Thank Him for giving you this desire. Thank Him that your desires are for your benefit. Thank Him for protecting and providing for what He put in your heart.

Ask Him if it is okay for you to come back to this vision, and ask how often you can. Get His permission on how to interact with this vision and what's appropriate for your present time. Is it okay? If so, how often? _____

Always keep in mind His kindness and goodness to give you this desire. Refer back to Jeremiah 29:11: He wants to prosper you. He wants to give you hope. He wants to give you a future. He wants to co-create your desires with you. Thank Him for this sweet time together and for His voice.

Express gratitude for God's willingness to request your obedience so He can take you towards this desire in your heart through your *yes* to Him.

_____
_____
_____

Every *yes* is an opportunity to move closer to the desires in your heart from Him. He wants to see you get there. He wants to see you arrive at living out your dreams. He will help you arrive by asking for your obedience. As you obey, you can grow into the person you need to be to live out that desire.

His requests are for our benefit. He always wants to promote us into what is highest and best for us. Give Him your *yes*; I promise you will not regret it. He will lead you into a fulfilled life beyond your wildest dreams. You can't even imagine the goodness of what's possible when you give Him your *yes*.

Declarations and Decrees

- I am aligned with obedience to my Heavenly Father.
- I know God is for me and looking to promote me.
- I trust God's requests of me.
- I trust myself to give God my *yes*.
- I allow obedience to my Heavenly Father to be on my breath.
- I know that His plans for me are good.
- I know God wants to prosper me.
- I believe that hope is my future.
- I surrender to the flow of the Holy Spirit's leading.
- I allow obedience to be a fluid part of my life.
- I have grace for saying *yes* to God.
- I know my desires are for my benefit and that God wants to deliver on those promises He placed inside me.

Write some more of your own here:
-
-

Below, take as long as you need to journal about all the ways shifting into obedience could propel your life forward. What is the Lord asking you to do in this season? Have you been hesitant to give your *yes*? Who could you become when you ease into this *yes*?

_____
_____
_____
_____

The Shift of Story

Many of us have stories we need to shift because we have stories we tell ourselves that keep us stuck, feeling overwhelmed, not good enough, etc. Those are the lying stories we need to rewrite. For example, for so long, the story I told myself was that *I didn't matter*. Eventually, I had to face the lie and own that I *did* matter, or why else would I be here? When I looked at the story of why I believed I didn't matter in the first place, I opened myself to seeing a different possibility. My story shifted. I stopped believing that life had to be hard. I started believing my life would work for me and serve who I was created to be. I shifted the stories I was believing about my life from crippling lies to hope-filled beliefs.

All of us also have a different kind of story: We carry powerful wisdom that is waiting to be unlocked through sharing life experiences we have been through and overcome. These experiences have given us authority to help someone else who's going through similar circumstances. Your life story matters; it has the power to make a great impact in the lives of others. For example, me showing up to write this book. I wrestled with it for years, but ultimately knew I had to finish it for others. I wanted my son to see that even from brokenness you can become whole. I never want him to question if his life matters or not like I did so many times. The answer is, yes, it does, so we have to show up to tell our stories and testimonies.

Identifying the stories we tell ourselves requires self-awareness. I placed the Shift of Story as one of the last sections because coming to terms with the lies we've believed, the false stories we've told ourselves, is hard. You've become more aware of yourself throughout this journey, and I believe you're ready to acknowledge the stories you've created that don't measure up to God's truth for you. It's never too late to lay those stories down and pick up His truth.

Ask Questions

Am I protecting or clinging to my false stories that keep me stuck and feeling small? If so, why is that?

_____
_____
_____
_____
_____

If someone presents a perspective or belief that contradicts what my stories say, do I feel threatened by it? Can I allow myself to hear what they have to say, or do I become defensive? When has this happened before?

Where do my stories keep me stuck in life?

Has trauma become my truth instead of what God says about me? What past trauma(s) has become my truth, and how can I reevaluate the "truth" of my stories?

Who do I need to become to believe the truth about myself?

If my life truly matters, what behaviors need an upgrade to demonstrate to the world around me that it does?

_____
_____
_____
_____
_____

Am I willing to sacrifice the stories that are holding me back from being the truest, most aligned and congruent version of who God created me to be?

_____
_____

Tangible Tools

A testimony is simply declaring and testifying the goodness of God in your life. I want you to write your testimony so you can document what God has done and keep your story alive. I want you to tell the story of trauma or pain in your own words. Write out all that you remember, and also what it made you believe and feel about yourself and your future. What did you make that situation mean about you?

Then, write down why you know the old story isn't truth. If you need help, begin to think of scriptures that express the opposite of those old beliefs. Below, journal the process of breaking the chain that connects the limiting beliefs of your old story to your potential.

What do you see? How does it feel? How does Jesus interact with you? What does it mean to you now to be free of those old beliefs? How will you share your story with the world around you? Who do you get to be now that you have released the burdened part of your life? What does this new level of freedom look like for you when you step out to share your story, to testify of His goodness?

_____
_____
_____
_____
_____
_____

The Sounds of His Voice

Joshua 2 (ESV)

And Joshua the son of Nun sent two men secretly from Shittim as spies, saying, "Go, view the land, especially Jericho." And they went and came into the house of a prostitute whose name was Rahab and lodged there. And it was told to the king of Jericho, "Behold, men of Israel have come here tonight to search out the land." Then the king of Jericho sent to Rahab, saying, "Bring out the men who have come to you, who entered your house, for they have come to search out all the land." But the woman had taken the two men and hidden them. And she said, "True, the men came to me, but I did not know where they were from. And when the gate was about to be closed at dark, the men went out. I do not know where the men went. Pursue them quickly, for you will overtake them." But she had brought them up to the roof and hid them with the stalks of flax that she had laid in order on the roof. So the men pursued after them on the way to the Jordan as far as the fords. And the gate was shut as soon as the pursuers had gone out.

Before the men lay down, she came up to them on the roof and said to the men, "I know that the LORD has given you the land, and that the fear of you has fallen upon us, and that all the inhabitants of the land melt away before you. For we have heard how the LORD dried up the water of the Red Sea before you when you came out of Egypt, and what you did to the two kings of the Amorites who were beyond the Jordan, to Sihon and Og, whom you devoted to destruction. And as soon as we heard it, our hearts melted, and there was no spirit left in any man because of you, for the LORD your God, he is God in the heavens above and on the earth beneath. Now then, please swear to me by the LORD that, as I have dealt kindly with you, you also will deal kindly with my father's house, and give me a sure sign that you will save alive my father and mother, my brothers and sisters, and all who belong to them, and deliver our lives from death." And the men said to her, "Our life for yours even to death! If you do not tell this business of ours, then when the LORD gives us the land we will deal kindly and faithfully with you."

Then she let them down by a rope through the window, for her house was built into the city wall, so that she lived in the wall. And she said to them, "Go into the hills, or the pursuers will encounter you, and hide there three days until the pursuers have returned. Then afterward you may go your way." The men said to her, "We will be guiltless with respect to this oath of yours that you have made us swear. Behold, when we come into the land, you shall tie this scarlet cord in the window through which you let us down, and you shall gather into your house your father and mother, your brothers, and all your father's household. Then if anyone goes out of the doors of your house into the street, his blood shall be on his own head, and we shall be guiltless. But if a hand is laid on anyone who is with you in the house, his blood shall be on our head. But if you tell this business of ours, then we shall be guiltless with respect to your oath that you have made us swear." And she said, "According to your words, so be it." Then she sent them away, and they departed. And she tied the scarlet cord in the window.

They departed and went into the hills and remained there three days until the pursuers returned, and the pursuers searched all along the way and found nothing. Then the two men returned. They came down from the hills and passed over and came to Joshua the son of Nun, and they told him all that had happened to them. And they said to Joshua, "Truly the LORD has given all the land into our hands. And also, all the inhabitants of the land melt away because of us."

What do I sense God is trying to show me or say to me in Joshua 2?

_____
_____
_____
_____
_____
_____
_____

What if we, like Rahab, could lay down our past, the things that didn't serve us, and take action on opportunities created to step into the potential the Lord has for us? Like Rahab, what could happen in my life if I got rid of my stories of fear and limitation?

_____
_____
_____
_____
_____
_____
_____

Learning Forward

Learning Forward Discovery: There is always a solution to the problems that get in the way of your dreams.

Your story is powerful. Your story is who you are – what you are made of, how you interact with the world, the legacy and impact you will leave when you're no longer here. I want you to know that both big and small things in life create your true story or the lying stories you believe.

I have lying stories attached to why *I can't* wear white. I also had lying stories attached to people, circumstances, sex, marriage, making money, and more. It's our choice how we view those things.

Maybe there were catastrophes around one of the subjects above for you too. Sometimes it's not about the major, catastrophic moments though (lies, sexual, verbal, physical, or spiritual abuse, etc.). Sometimes it's the tiny and seemingly non-catastrophic moments that feel the easiest to believe (like not being able to wear white).

Say you're eating at In 'n Out Burger while wearing a brand-new white dress. You promised yourself white would be okay to wear, even though the past has proven over and over that *you just can't wear white*. As you bite into your burger and the "special sauce" orange spread drips down, splattering all over that brand new dress, you have choices…

1. Fall into old thinking, proving yourself right once again that white isn't your color, no matter how badly you want to wear it.
2. Curse loudly, as though that will change anything.
3. Rapidly Google search how to remove stains and make it happen; reframe your brain to know there is always a solution to the dreams in your heart.

What response would I typically have? _____

You can be confident in knowing who you are and how to go after the dream in your heart…even after terror, trauma, and chaos. I want to see you have such high awareness of your value that small happenings in your day don't stick to you, but you move through them fluidly and with ease. I want this because your confidence will give you boldness to know that you matter, and when you know you matter, you are likely to tell your story to help others have breakthroughs as well! It's a beautiful cycle – moving from lying stories to telling life stories in order to empower or encourage another.

Where in my life do I desire more boldness? What story do I need to get rid of for that to happen?
_____
_____
_____
_____
_____

Breathwork/Meditation

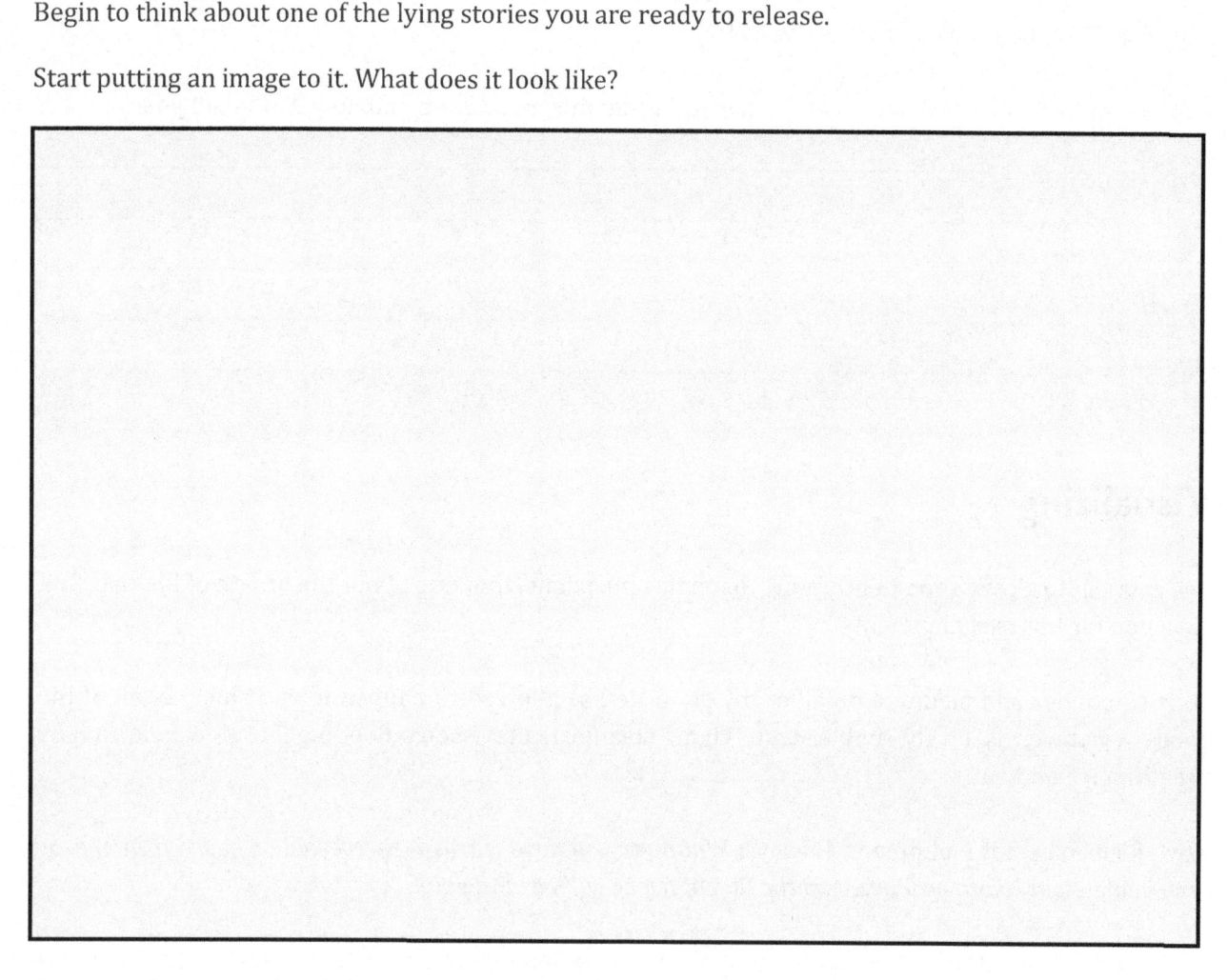

Begin to think about one of the lying stories you are ready to release.

Start putting an image to it. What does it look like?

Once you have visualized the story, imagine it chained to your potential, dragging it down. Picture yourself going to the chains. Invite Jesus to be there with you. Jesus is Truth. Ask Him to help you tell the chains they cannot hold your potential to this story any longer. Tell the chains this story no longer serves you and is a lie.

Release – it's time to see yourself removing the chains. Maybe you want to karate chop them or you use a key to unlock them. Whatever your method, I want YOU to remove the chains between your limiting story and your powerful life story that is full of potential.

Now, hand the chains to Jesus. In your own words, tell Him *thank you* for being with you in this revelatory moment of greatness. Repent for allowing the false story to be told again and again, keeping you from your purpose. Ask Him for a deeper revelation of your value here on earth. Surrender to Him.

He is kind and gentle, full of grace and mercy.

Allow yourself to be captivated by Him in this moment. Follow His lead in whatever He wants in this moment. Share this time of intimacy with Him.

Take a moment to write down what happened during this meditation and how it affected you.

_____
_____
_____
_____
_____

Visualizing

Get yourself to a cozy spot. Gently start to inhale and exhale, thinking about the breath of life that God gave you for this exact moment.

Start to ponder and meditate on all of the good He has allowed to happen in your life. Let all of the good—whatever is lovely, noble, true, right, steadfast, etc.—start flooding in. Slow and steady breathing, in and out.

Now, focus on what Philippians 4:9 says: *Whatever you have learned or received or heard from me, or seen in me—put it into practice. And the God of peace will be with you.*

Paul used his life story to encourage others to do the same, to let them know that they should be confident in sharing their story as well. As you continue breathing, imagine what it would be like if you said *yes* to sharing your life story, knowing it does matter and will impact those listening. How much influence can your story bring when you tell it to glorify God and expand His Kingdom? What if it's to just one person, is that worth it?

Let your breath fill with His peace; let your life story rise inside of you, the testimony of His goodness in your life. Just as Paul was imprisoned and used his story to spread the Gospel, how can you use your story to impact others?

Keep breathing until you feel there is clarity to shift you from broken, lying stories into freedom to tell your life story. Stay comfy and keep breathing; think about all that is good.

What did you see and experience during this visualization?

_____
_____
_____
_____

Declarations and Decrees

- I trust the process of healing.
- I allow myself to release stories that no longer serve me.
- I am open to seeing the holes in my beliefs so I can shore them up with truth instead of lies.
- I allow myself to release limiting thoughts and embrace empowering ones.
- I have clarity in my next steps.
- I see my true value.
- I am allowed to do what is right for me.
- I am willing to lay down old patterns for new ones.
- I am willing to see and create opportunities for myself.
- I tell my life story to empower and encourage others.
- I use the authority gained in my life experiences to help others avoid unnecessary pain.
- I matter.
- My life story is a testament of His goodness.
- My life story matters.

Write some more of your own here:
-
-

Below, take as long as you need to journal about changing the stories that hold you back from being the truest, most aligned and congruent version of who God created you to be. What is the one story you're believing right now that keeps you from being your most authentic and congruent self? If you laid this story to rest, how aligned would you feel within yourself and with God?

_____
_____

The Shift of Celebration

You've acknowledged that what got you to this place in life won't be what gets you to the next. You've been ready to grow. You've faced painful emotions in this journey – uncomfortable thoughts and feelings about who you are and who you want to be. You're doing the work.

And now, it's time to celebrate! You have everything needed to be successful built into you. You're developing skills and honing gifts and refining desires. You are nourishing yourself and nurturing the seeds of influence planted in you by your Creator. The more you celebrate who you are, the miracle of your life, the more fluidly you move through your life. Less garbage from life will stick to you, and when it does, you release it much more quickly. Celebration is your key to seeing your #holyshift unrestrained and with ultimate transformation.

When I wasn't fully healed, my view of God and His love for me was skewed. I believed whispers of hell came from Heaven. I was so confused! The Bible says there is no condemnation for those in Christ Jesus (John 3:18), but I didn't feel that way. I had glimpses of who I could become, but I didn't think I deserved my hopes and dreams coming true.

I also compared myself to others all the time. I would tell myself things like, *I'm too simple...no, too complex. I'm not smart enough. I'm the wrong size, the wrong color, the wrong religion... I'm the wrong* fill-in-the-blank. Every time I compared myself to another person or to what I thought I should be, a little part of me died. Dreams faded and contentment settled in.

When I finally heard Heaven asking me, "Who are you?" I let go of comparison. I understood God wanted me to know myself so He could champion me into greatness and into the fulfillment of the dreams He'd placed in my heart. He knows me and my dreams better than I do. You've read all throughout this book how patterns of trauma foster lies we tell ourselves, and they also embed doubt and disbelief that our dreams are of God. But as God champions us into greatness, He celebrates us. It's time we join Him in celebration!

Celebrate your dreams. Celebrate your current position. Celebrate your mess and your flaws. The lies have served to justify our belief that we won't see our dreams come true. But celebrating through our shifts of Awareness, Support, Perseverance, Gratitude, Self, Obedience, and Story fortifies and seals faith that our dreams *are* coming true right NOW. We celebrate the journey!

Ask Questions

Do I have any traditions that help me celebrate well? How can I use traditions to celebrate my accomplishments and successes?

_____
_____
_____
_____
_____

What family traditions would I *like* to start observing? Are there any traditions I should shift away from?

_____
_____
_____
_____
_____

Imagine planning a celebration event for myself. What might it include? What would I decorate with? Would there be special food? Who would I invite and why?

_____
_____
_____
_____
_____

Is there a celebratory ritual I could include in my daily routine? What is a simple, meaningful activity to commemorate my growth and who I am?

_____
_____

Do I find it easy to celebrate others? What kind of accomplishments and growth do others have that offend me? What kind of accomplishments or growth in others inspires me?

___

What feelings do I associate with celebrations? Are there any unpleasant feelings, judgmental attitudes, or memories regarding celebrations that I need to release?

___

Where have I wanted a celebration to be present, but it just isn't? Am I called to be part of that solution? If so, how can I help bring celebration into more parts of everyday life?

___

What was my favorite celebration as a kid? A holiday, a birthday, a graduation, or something else entirely? What did those celebrations stir inside of me? What do I wish they stirred? How can I bring those feelings into my everyday life now?

___

Does celebrating others help me feel childlike giddiness? How can I celebrate others in such a way that they feel the love?

_____
_____
_____
_____

Tangible Tools

Celebrations honor people and build them up. Celebrations testify to the goodness all around. Celebration helps solidify the accomplishments of a season. Celebrations advance us and pull our future into the now. Celebration brings life, it brings joy, and people need more of it in their lives...so do you. Celebration can be as simple as journaling, writing a letter, posting on social media, or going out to a nice dinner. But what about a party?

Party ideas:

- Wine and cheese
- Game night
- Potluck
- 80's theme (or any decade theme)
- A come-as-you'll-be party (ten years from now, who will you be? Ask all of your guests to come as themselves in ten years from now)
- A movie night party, popcorn bar and all
- Ice cream sundae party
- Taco night
- Pizza night
- Any specific type of food or drink night
- Murder mystery dinner
- Any sport party
- Arts and crafts party
- Painting party
- Luau-style party
- A book/tea/coffee exchange party
- Beer and burgers
- Fondue
- A progressive dinner/dessert party with friends or neighbors

Should I throw a party? If so, what kind? Who should I invite? What action steps can I take to make this a reality?

_____
_____
_____
_____
_____

How would I want people to feel at my party? How would I want to feel at my party?

_____
_____
_____
_____
_____

What does a celebration look like to me? Draw it!

Tag me @hollipeel on Instagram when you celebrate so I can celebrate with you!

The Sounds of His Voice

Acts 17:25
...He supplies life and breath and all things to every living being.

When it comes to celebration, what is God speaking to me through this verse?

_____
_____
_____
_____
_____
_____
_____

Learning Forward

Learning Forward Discovery: How do you see an elephant? One light at a time.

Often, I find myself having wonderful creative ideas, and then seeing a similar theme show up in other places and from other people. This makes me feel down on myself and a little defeated, like I missed my chance. But, I've realized we all see and know in part; we all have something to contribute even if our contributions seem similar. When you recognize a theme among your unique ideas and things happening around you, know that God is on the move, revealing a message to His people. Each of us receives and communicates the message differently, so we can't allow comparison to stop us from communicating in our own way. It takes many people sharing the same message in many different ways for all to hear. It's like being in a large, dark room with an elephant in the center. We all have tiny flashlights and can only light up our piece of it. When we all take part in discovering together, the message is unified and revealed in fullness.

The Shift of Celebration is for you *and* for those around you. You get to move into being more of yourself and away from comparison, and this opens the door for you to show up for others in their lives. You can start to shine the flashlight on their "elephant" to help them see the part only you can see. Help them celebrate that part of them, and you will see how contagious celebration is. You will start to step into more and more breakthroughs in your own life as you celebrate together!

Celebration is a key from the Lord. If celebration can shift us from stagnant and stuck to enjoyment and success, and it can do this for others too, who can I help celebrate?

_____
_____
_____
_____

Breathwork/Meditation

Take a deep breath in - the kind of breath that fills your whole body. The kind of deep, long breath that inflates your whole chest, all the way down to your belly button.

Slow. Steady. Calming. Deep. Celebratory for your life.

The Holy Spirit is called the Breath of God. As you breathe, picture every cell in your body being filled anew with the Holy Spirit. Every DNA strand in your body comes online in a new way. Notice the fresh new thing He is doing inside you.

Let your breath thank Him for the joy He gives you, the joy He is on the inside of you, the joy He is as He spills out into your everyday life.

What fresh new thing is He doing in me?

_____
_____
_____
_____
_____

Visualizing

Hold out your hands, palms up. In your right hand, I want you to imagine who you are now – the strengths you have, the flaws you have, the mistakes you have made, all of the things that you represent today, right now. Hold those things. In your left hand, imagine all of the dreams, desires, hopes, and aspirations you have – the person that you could only dream of becoming. Let that settle in and warm you a little. Maybe see if, with each breath you take, you can feel it fill your fingertips and warm your palms as you hold both parts of you. Who you are *and* who you want to become.

Now that you have your left and right hands full of the vision of today and tomorrow, I want you to thank who you were yesterday and the day before and the day before. Without that person being willing to show up, to learn, to change, to grow, you might not be the person you are today.

Am I still holding a little judgment for myself in my right hand? _____

If so, practice this daily, and the judgment will start to weaken. You will begin to feel more and more gratitude for the person you were and what that version of you went through to get you here *today*. Tomorrow, celebrate what the today version of you was able to accomplish to get you there...do you see the pattern? Be always willing to thank yesterday's you, celebrate today's you, and dream with tomorrow's you. One step, one day, one celebratory moment at a time.

Describe how this visualization affected your perspective about yourself.

_____
_____
_____
_____
_____
_____

Declarations and Decrees

- I celebrate myself each and every day.
- It is easy for me to celebrate my uniqueness.
- It is easy for me to celebrate others and their success.
- I celebrate easily and often because the Celebrator lives inside of me.
- I allow joy and laughter into my daily life.
- Celebration finds me and surrounds me.
- Celebration brings me life and deeper levels of joy.
- I allow Heavenly Father to celebrate me.
- I allow Holy Spirit to lead me to celebrate others.
- My celebration of others helps them feel important and loved.
- My celebration leads people into a greater understanding of who Jesus is.
- I embrace celebrating, and celebration embraces me.
- I relish celebration.

Write some more of your own here:
-
-

Below, take as long as you need to journal about all the things in your life that are worthy of celebrating and how you can incorporate celebration more.

What's Next?

I'm so thrilled you've chosen to take action and *Own Your Shift* by using this workbook and journal. Now, I'd like to include my whole last chapter from my main book in case you don't have it yet. If you have a business or have considered having a business, this chapter is especially for you.

Back in 2018, I started getting Facebook ads for this guy named Pedro Adao. I was honestly turned off by his ads and annoyed that they popped in my feed so often. At one time, I even used the "hide this for 30 days" feature Facebook offered. This was a super fragile season of life; our business was just getting back off of the ground after a natural disaster as well as some personnel complications. I was also working hard to get my dōTerra network marketing business up and running. All in on that business, I was sprinting toward creating an income that would help our family. So, "annoying" Facebook ads were the last thing I wanted to see on my feed.

I am so thankful that God knows more than I do (LOL) and for His divine intervention and wisdom. The 30 days must have expired because my Facebook feed continued to show me ads from this Pedro Adao guy; this time it was for an event he was hosting in person, just an hour drive from my house. I honestly ignored the ad for weeks, but at the last minute decided to spend $195 on a ticket and attend in person. I'd go just for the first night because my favorite prophetic speaker, Kris Vallotton, was going to be there. I told myself that I would go and gave myself permission to leave if this Pedro guy annoyed me as much in person as he did in the Facebook ads.

The crazy thing is, as soon as I bought the ticket, I had a message in my Facebook Direct Messages from "Pedro Adao" instantly I thought, *this must be a bot or something automated...* But no, it was really him. We ended up having a conversation about what I did and why I was coming. I was shocked that he actually took time to message me. So, my heart started to soften towards him; *maybe he isn't just out for my money after all.*

I showed up at the event and was instantly drawn in; the staff and volunteers were so kind and welcoming. I was letting my walls down moment by moment through every person I met and conversation I had. The first session came around, and it was Pedro and his beautiful wife Suzette who took the stage. I was shocked at how normal they seemed, not like the normal "guru" types of people who I had purchased courses from in the past.

Kris Vallotton got up and spoke; it was amazing as usual, but this time I heard him talk about entrepreneurship in ways I had not heard him discuss before. You see, at this time, I was convinced that I was not an entrepreneur. Who knows why, because all of the clues led to me being a full-fledged entrepreneur. I loved solving problems, being creative, and innovative; I loved starting new projects and constantly had new ideas and downloads. I just didn't know that was the spirit of entrepreneurship and I could learn it as a skill and apply it to my life! To me it felt more like a nuisance – always spinning my wheels, not really moving forward. Little did I know that what Kris (and later Pedro) talked about in regards to entrepreneurship made my heart come alive and start to sing.

Later that night, Pedro talked about love and how love was the best business strategy. He said, "Those who love the most will always win." When he said this, something inside of me sparked and caught fire. It was the language I had been looking for to describe how I felt on the inside, how I operated, and what I wanted to grow deeper in: LOVE as a business strategy. What a remarkable concept!

Needless to say, I decided to stay for the rest of the conference. On day two, I had fully surrendered myself to the Lord and whatever He wanted to do in my life while I was there. Well, Pedro invited everyone in the room into a 12-month training program. The problem I saw was the price tag. We were just starting to come out of a very hard financial season, and spending that kind of money, no matter the value, didn't seem like a wise call. But God. I knew we had a credit card with just the right amount of space, but I was honestly terrified. Still, I knew this was the step of trust I needed to take in my relationship with God. Normally, I relied on my husband to help me make these kinds of decisions; normally, I would call and have a conversation so we could be in agreement on big decisions like this, but I had to trust that God was doing something in my life and leading me to trust Him more deeply. I said yes to Pedro's training program that day, and as a matter of fact, was the first person in line to enroll.

You might be wondering why I am sharing this level of detail, and if you're still here, you most likely know it's because I'm talking to a part of your heart that's hungry for how this story unfolds.

Pedro's invitation from the stage to join his 12-month program was a bonus, and this bonus was what stood out most to me. It was worth a mere $130, but it was the "promise" that came with it that truly intrigued me. Pedro was going to give the first 100 people who joined a YETI microphone because, as he said, "Our voices matter." Honestly, my mind went on a tangent after that part. God had already been whispering to me about my voice – about the stories I needed to tell, about the things I needed to say, about the life I had lived and the lessons I had learned that needed to be shared.

It really impacted me, because earlier in 2018, God woke me from a dead sleep and told me to start writing out a story about an experience in my life (you read it earlier in this very book). After I typed the story out, God told me to write a book. I knew I'd sat on that assignment since February and did nothing, and now here I was in October. Pedro was an author; he had the authority to teach me how to do that, and now he was talking about the importance of my voice. I didn't think my voice was important, but God did. He knew when I heard Pedro talk about this YETI bonus it would start me on the path to birthing this very book (and more to come).

In that season, I felt overwhelm, loneliness, lack, confusion, and hunger; I was so hungry for a breakthrough into what I knew life with the King should feel like. Little did I know that the breakthrough would come through my *yes*. Little did I know that my circumstances would not change until I did what I advocate for in this book: taking ownership of our lives, taking ownership of our shifts, taking ownership of our growth so we can partner with God for our expansion.

My troubles did not go away overnight, but I did start seeing instant changes. Our storage facility occupancy revenue brought in an additional $4,000 in one month, which we could only tie to God's faithfulness in response to my obedience. I started to experience more peace, and I showed up as a more present mom and loving wife. Why do those things matter as an entrepreneur? Well, if you are a female entrepreneur, then you know the power and importance of being a mom and wife. We can easily carry guilt about not living up to our best version of those things because of our business.

So, things were moving in a great direction. Michael was on board and supportive because I asked for his support rather than his permission to do this. He saw in me what God saw in me; he knew the potential and was so excited to see me taking action on my Kingdom assignment – even if I didn't know exactly what it was then. I also had God's permission, and I even gave myself permission.

Again, why am I telling you all of this?

I want you to know that if you're an entrepreneur or have felt the calling to be one, you are not alone. There are tools to help you; tools relevant to today's marketing and business strategy AND with God as the center. His principles can lead and guide you on how to show up to do business.

I want to see you succeed in the ways that I was able to. After I joined 100X, so much of my life started coming together. I started to see areas of my life converge at crucial intersections, allowing me to see more of who God wanted to be for me in my life and how He wanted me to show up: as my authentic and powerful self.

If you fast forward a few months, I went to another one of Pedro's conferences. This time it was in Texas, and upon my return home, I had an offer to join Pedro's team. I have a powerful story of God's goodness in how this unfolded, but I said yes to another opportunity from God through Pedro. Now, I work full time for Pedro, own storage investment properties, use my dōTerra oils, and kick booty as a mom and wife. Don't get me wrong; I have hard days, but the moral of the story is you have no idea what one *yes* to an invitation from God can do in your life. Maybe you do? Maybe you have a similar yes can pinpoint that catapulted your life forward, just like this did for me.

To bring it full circle, God told me to write a book; I put it on the shelf because I didn't feel qualified. Then, I heard Pedro talk about the power of my voice and said yes to the invitation to join 100X. I started working for Pedro as part of his team, finding my voice in a way I had no idea was possible, and now I am a published author who's on camera regularly in front of thousands and thousands of people.

Who knew it would take my willingness to do some hard things like get uncomfortable, take ownership of my choices, and shift into the growth of who God knew I could be from day one? God knew.

If you are intrigued to learn more about this, Pedro and I have created a special video for you. You can see it now at:

www.holliandpedro.com

Here are some other ways this video is for you, just in case you don't see yourself in my story. Do you feel pain in any of these areas of your life right now?

- Maybe you read this book and realize your emotions and feelings are often more than you know how to manage.
- Maybe you are trying to run a business and are often triggered by your employees or customers.
- Maybe you feel the pain and frustration of a lack of financial security in your life.
- Maybe you are identifying the call and importance of launching the dream inside of your heart.

Whatever it is, I believe God is putting His finger on that area as an invitation for you to go deeper. There is a level of breakthrough and authority just waiting for your yes.

Ask Him how He sees your situation and if this book's content contains an opportunity you have needed. Maybe this is an invitation, just like it was to me, into the next adventure God wants to take you on.

God is always calling us up, so ask Him what your next steps are into the more of Him. How can you partner with Him in a more tangible way to see the dream and desires of your heart come to pass?

If you have made it this far, you are one of those people who is hungry for more, one of those people who'll never stop growing, one who is willing to identify the pain and let it heal to take you to new levels.

This most likely also means you have so much life experience that there are wells of wisdom, knowledge, and breakthroughs inside of you, waiting to come out.

You have overcome much, and all of the pain and growth you have been through has been for you; it has developed your character and made you stronger. But it's not meant to be self-focused pain. In fact, I believe it was for your growth and for your good in order to use that pain to help others uplevel into the greatness God has called them to as well.

When we experience pain and then a breakthrough but keep it to ourselves, it is self-focused and not what we should aspire to. There are so many more promises for us and others when we use our life experiences to help uplevel all those around us.

God wants to meet so much more than just our basic needs. Are you ready to explore what that looks like for you and your walk with God?

Head to www.holliandpedro.com to learn more. I believe in you and the value that you carry. You matter!

XOXO,
Holli

What next steps will draw me closer to Him?

About the Author

Just like you, Holli Peel goes by many names and wears many different hats in life; names like. friend, aunt, entrepreneur, sister, dreamer, lover, and more. However, the titles she considers to be the greatest are Wife to her husband Michael of 15+ years and Mom to her son Micah.

You may have seen her with pom poms, cheering you along on a Zoom call as the official "100X Cheerleader!" After joining the 100X Academy as a student in 2018, she quickly became a core team member, working closely alongside Pedro Adao. Fast forward to today, she still serves powerfully and leads this number one, on-fire community for Kingdom entrepreneurs as the 100X Community Manager.

During her time with 100X, she has personally helped Pedro and team serve more than 5,000 high-performing clients, played a role in generating $30M+ in revenue alongside the 828 team, and impacted hundreds of thousands of lives through Pedro's industry-changing Challenge Model. In her personal business ventures, Holli is a six-figure earner and has co-created a multi-million-dollar investment portfolio.

After all her success, there is still one thing on Holli's to-do list: getting YOU to believe in yourself! One of her deepest desires is to help anyone she interacts with see their true value so they can live their life to the fullest and connect to their calling.

Please visit:

www.HolliandPedro.com

Connect with Holli on Instagram:

@hollipeel

Exclusive Publishing for Kingdom Entrepreneurs

www.100XPublishing.com

Made in the USA
Middletown, DE
16 November 2022